A Publication of the Harvard Negotiation Project

Brian Ganson, Editor

BEYOND MACHIAVELLI

Tools for Coping with Conflict

▼

Roger Fisher
Elizabeth Kopelman
Andrea Kupfer Schneider

Harvard University Press
Cambridge, Massachusetts
London, England
1994

To our students,
from whom we have learned so much

Library of Congress Cataloging-in-Publication Data
Fisher, Roger, 1922–
Beyond Machiavelli : tools for coping with conflict /
by Roger Fisher, Elizabeth Kopelman, Andrea Kupfer Schneider
p.   cm.
ISBN 0-674-06916-1
1. Pacific settlement of international disputes.
2. International relations. 3. Conflict management.
I. Kopelman, Elizabeth. II. Schneider, Andrea Kupfer. III. Title.
JX4473.F57   1994
327.1′6—dc20

Preface

The three authors of this book have been working together on these ideas, at Harvard University and in the real world, for some time. Much of the stimulus for writing them down was an undergraduate course at Harvard entitled Coping with International Conflict (CWIC). Roger, a member of the Law School faculty, taught that course first alone and then with Bruce Patton, who over fifteen years has moved from studying as an undergraduate to teaching as the Thaddeus R. Beal Lecturer on Law. Bruce also serves as the deputy director of the Harvard Negotiation Project, a research activity devoted to improving both ideas about negotiation and their implementation in the world at large.

Liz and Andrea, while students at the Law School, were teaching fellows and section leaders for CWIC, and then each, in turn, served as Head Teaching Fellow for the course. Both before and after obtaining a degree from the Law School, each was active in the Negotiation Project. All three of us have also been involved in the work of the Conflict Management Group, a nonprofit consulting firm set up by some of Roger's former students with his help, which offers training and advice in conflicts, primarily international ones, that involve political, social, ethnic, and other such issues. When dealing with conflicts discussed in this book, one or more of us was typically wearing an academic or nonprofit hat.

The CWIC course was concerned strictly with intergovernmental disputes, terrorist acts, and other nongovernmental clashes of international concern. Time and again our students were pleased to discover that an energetic undergraduate was able to produce an idea of interest to real-world decisionmakers dealing with real-world conflicts. But more surprising to us were the reports we got from our students, almost daily, that the "international" tools they were learning were immediately relevant to disputes in their daily lives, whether with roommates, parents, landlords, summer employers, or automobile mechanics. The basic questions were the same: Whom would you like to influence? How do they see their choice? How might you change it?

While this book is mostly about international conflict, based on our teaching experience we are confident that the relevance of these ideas to other kinds of disputes will be clear. If you use and adapt the tools in this book in a new way, or if you do not find them relevant to the kinds of conflict in which you are involved, please drop us a line at the Harvard Negotiation Project, Harvard Law School, Cambridge, Massachusetts 02138, and let us know. Our purpose is to keep learning.

— Cambridge, October 1993

Contents

Introduction:
Why This Book?

Conflict is a growth industry. As our world becomes increasingly interdependent, more and more people bump into one another more and more often. In a rapidly changing international context, a solution that seemed adequate last month may be out of date next week. The United States' goal in 1980 of strengthening Saddam Hussein against Iran was made obsolete by Iraq's 1990 occupation of Kuwait. Trade wars, global warming, ethnic conflict, and exploding numbers of refugees are all problems that demand something more than one-shot solutions.

The world today is not necessarily the world that has to be. Who would have thought, forty years ago, that relations between France and Germany, Egypt and Israel, or the United States and Japan would ever be as they are now? Who could have foreseen, even a short time ago, that the political landscape in Central Europe would be anything like what it is today? Even one year from now, relations between the United States and China, between Iran and Iraq, among the five Central American nations, or among the nations of the European Community may also look completely different.

We believe that it is worth thinking systematically about what is wrong with the world, how it might look if it were better, and, in particular, what specific steps people — or any one person — can take to improve it. It is not that people lack the desire for a world that works well — a world at peace in which democracy and human rights flourish — nor lack a foreign policy that favors such a world. Most difficulties occur at the much more pragmatic level of ends and means, of what might be called nuts and bolts.

International conflicts are not being handled as well as they might be. As we review a typical day's headlines, it is apparent that nations tend to react to the actions of others, rather than act in forward-looking ways to achieve their own ends. Governments frequently show more concern for having the correct attitude toward a problem or for making an elegant statement about it than for bringing about beneficial change. Too often, foreign policy decisionmakers fail to focus on the decisions of those they are trying to influence. There is a shortage of theory on how conflicts ought to be handled, and a shortage of practical skill in bringing that theory to bear on the real world.

This book seeks to address both shortages. It lays out some tools for conflict analysis, and some practical applications of these tools that can help refine problem-solving skills. Instead of just asking why things work — or don't — we ask how individuals can affect the way things work. Instead of just learning how other people get things done, we will consider ways that people both inside and outside of government — CEOs, scientists, lobbyists, academics, journalists, diplomats, church leaders, university students — might themselves influence international events.

1

Look Forward
with a Purpose

On television and in the newspapers, we see the anguished face of a Croatian father as he is told of the death of his son. We have seen that expression before: on the face of a Sudanese woman, a Palestinian teenager, and a Korean student. Day in and day out, the abstract topic of "international conflict" is played out as moving — or numbing — examples of individual pain. Although interested in the problems of the wider world, we sometimes skip the international section of our daily paper, or only skim the depressing headlines and glance at the horrifying photographs. Why are we being shown these images? Even if we wanted to take action, just what are we supposed to do about it?

An important assumption underlying this book is the idea that our actions, as individuals, can make a difference. A generation ago foreign affairs was an arcane and specialized field, the preserve of a few expert enthusiasts, much like birdwatching or stamp collecting. The fall of the Berlin Wall, the collapse of communism in the former Soviet Union, famine in Somalia, and the new intensity of debate around trade, aid, open borders, and ethnic conflict have sparked an interest in the field among non-specialists, and called many to service who never before saw themselves as players. And it's about time. The foreign policy establishment needs fresh thinking. A decisionmaker with responsibility for foreign policy or national security should no longer be limited to the same well-established coterie of pundits, academics, and fellow-players.

In this book we have adopted the style of a handbook or how-to manual, to encourage an activist and problem-solving approach among people who like to — or must — think about tough problems. This book is meant to be used, not only by those in positions of global influence, but also by a teacher organizing a meeting of the school committee, by a corporate executive designing a new approach to a management problem, or by a member of a citizens' lobbying group concerned about toxic waste disposal. Many of our examples are drawn from foreign relations because that is where our primary interests, and many of the biggest problems, lie. That has also been the source of some of our first-hand experience at the Harvard Negotiation Project and the Conflict Management Group. Other examples are drawn from experiences with which many readers will be familiar, from business and law to personal relationships.

When one is faced with any conflict, we believe it is more useful to think about a good *process* for handling a flow of problems than to think about "solving" a particular problem once and for all. In fluid and turbulent times, it is better to think in terms of coping with conflicts than resolving them.

Understanding our task as conflict management rather than conflict resolution is a paradigm shift — away from a conception of conflict and negotiation that stresses static substantive solutions and toward an approach that stresses the power of process. Rarely is a conflict intractable simply because no one has a good idea of how things ought to be. There are dozens of plans floating around offering new "answers" to the crisis in Bosnia or the ethnic minority problems of the former Soviet Union. In most cases the difficulty lies not in a lack of potential substantive options but in the failure to design, negotiate, and pursue a process that moves us forward from where we are now to where we would like to be.

The approach we discuss in the following pages gets results. It enables us to generate tangible things we could actually show to another person, to illustrate the basis for our current thinking on a problem and to persuade him to take a more productive course of action. For example, following guidelines outlined in the chapters to come, we can create:

- a *checklist* of steps to analyze a conflict;
- a *set of analytic tools,* to figure out why a conflict has not been settled and to develop new approaches;
- an *action plan* including, for example, materials we would like to have in hand in order to present our ideas persuasively to another party, such as
  - a two-page digest of our proposal,
  - one page of "talking points" that can be easily understood, and
  - a to-do list of who will do what tomorrow morning.

We are not looking for a perfect solution. We do not assume that all conflicts can be settled peacefully or that all negotiations will — or should — lead to agreement. Nor do we assume that we operate in a rational world. On the contrary, we are trying to reason about conflict with all its irrational components. That patients may be irrational is hardly grounds for doctors to be so. And even the fact that doctors get tired and emotional, or stop thinking clearly, hardly means that they should. The more often reason produces good answers, the more likely it is to be called upon.

What we call "international relations" is actually the cumulative effect of hundreds of daily decisions. A key element of understanding why things happen is to know why generals, terrorists, foreign ministers, and others make decisions as they do. To gather knowledge and bring it to bear in such a way that the conduct of foreign affairs is less dangerous and less costly, we need to get inside the heads of those involved.

To take a closer look at the decisionmaking process, we start by breaking it down into two parts. First, we look at *who* needs to make a decision to take constructive action. Where are choices weighed and decisions made, and by which individuals, committees, and departments? Next, we ask what is the best advice someone could give to those decisionmakers? This book concentrates on what to do in order to develop the best professional advice and target it effectively.

Advise a Prince

Machiavelli's *Prince* is a powerful book that is still read after almost five hundred years. This is so not because the prince for whom Machiavelli was writing followed his advice or even read the book. The book is powerful because Machiavelli asked a powerful question: What advice would you give a prince? Whether you are a member of an influential elite with access to world leaders or simply an ordinary citizen with access to a daily newspaper, we encourage you, in this book, to step into Machiavelli's shoes by targeting an individual decisionmaker — a "prince" — and developing ideas that might persuade that decisionmaker to make a better choice on one issue. Generating advice — even if it is only hypothetical — is the best way to think rigorously about difficult problems.

Generating advice also provides a way to relate the wisdom of different disciplines. It is meaningless to ask whether military or economic considerations are more important in a given conflict without a particular choice in mind. Once a particular decision is seen as an open question, we can consider how military and economic considerations might best be taken into account. There is no answer to the question whether law or psychiatry is more important, but if a lawyer and a psychiatrist are asked to advise a judge on the sentencing of a juvenile, we have immediately presented the different disciplines with a common question. It becomes possible to produce advice drawing on both forms of expertise.

Every baseball fan knows the satisfaction that comes from understanding the game well enough to second-guess decisions made by the professionals. Fans who know enough to say what advice they would have given the manager, or what advice they would now give the catcher or the runner on first, will enjoy the game more than spectators who can simply describe what is going on.

The practical task of generating advice allows us individually and collectively to consider ideas with greater precision. We can clarify different objectives and analyze the best ways of meeting them. If two physicists spend their time predicting what kind of an airplane a manufacturer is going to build, their talents are not being well used. And they will end up knowing far less about aerodynamics than if they spent their time figuring out what advice they would give to the manufacturer that would allow him to build at low cost, for example, a cargo plane which could land and take off from a short runway. Even if the airplane manufacturer does not follow the advice of our two physicists, it is still valuable for them to spend their time generating good advice as a tool for their own research. Focusing on the task of producing hypothetical or real advice provides us with criteria for relevance — our advice has to be relevant to somebody for some purpose.

Most people are not CEOs or secretaries of state, but many people, in the course of their daily work, make decisions with the potential to change the world — a little. More of us could make a difference by first defining a manageable problem and then formulating a process for handling it. Working through our professional contacts, elected representatives, or volunteer agencies, perhaps we could offer advice to an influential person in the role of an informal adviser. Certainly we could all improve our skill at acting as our own Machiavelli in coping with situations where we ourselves have a decision to make, whether local or global. The goal of generating the best possible professional advice is even more relevant when we are generating advice to ourselves.

Beyond Predictability

Most university courses and scholarly texts approach international relations from the standpoint of a spectator. They seek to produce an explanatory structure — some bigger picture that orders events as part of a pattern. They tend to operate on the assumption that hard data are better than soft, and that quantifiable information has greater merit than qualitative information. Influenced no doubt by the physical sciences, an international relations specialist is likely to look for objective facts and strong correlations. Our very vocabulary suggests the importance we attribute to numerical data: Things "don't count" unless we can count them.

Research driven by hard data tends to direct our attention to body counts, military hardware, and foreign aid dollars. It implicitly suggests that the value of research lies in the extent to which it enables us to predict something that is going to happen, or to show why a past event was inevitable. But, as the best experts in international relations have learned, the more that research focuses our attention on what is predictable, the more it diverts our attention from those things we can affect. If we want knowledge in order to improve the world, then predictability is the wrong standard. We need to turn from what is inevitable to those things we can change.

While the approach of academic researchers often produces merely elegant postmortems, commentators and pundits who criticize foreign policy choices are also missing an opportunity to help the world manage its problems. Newspapers, magazines, and elected political figures regularly demand the wrong kind of performance from officials concerned with foreign affairs. Critics ask the players to play to the grandstand. They judge performance by the consistency of policy statements, by the political correctness of attitudes, or by short-term effect on popularity. Rarely do they judge performance by results. A decision on the partition of Bosnia along ethnic lines is judged not by its impact on what happens there but by its effect on public opinion polls at home.

When we go to buy an automobile, if we insist only on flashy trim, maximum horsepower, and a comfortable ride, we can expect an automobile that is unsafe at any speed. When we judge foreign policy, if we insist only on flashy public statements, maximum military power, and our own comfortable domestic agenda, we can expect a foreign policy that is also unsafe at any speed.

Where a situation is personal and close at hand, we often

realize that performance is more important than public relations. We would be suspicious if a doctor were currying favor with a parent rather than attending to a sick child. We do not ask a mechanic for consistent policy statements of his attitude toward different makes of automobiles. We want him to diagnose a difficulty and get to work on it. And when the mechanic does so, he is not ignoring his constituency; he is being responsive to public demand. It is simply that in such cases the public is more enlightened.

If our purpose as potential advisers to international decision-makers is to improve the caliber of criticism, we need to move beyond predictions and unconstructive criticism. We need to look at a particular choice somebody faces and ask how things might be better done. In order to criticize a baseball manager for replacing a pitcher, it is not enough to say that it is unusual to replace a pitcher in the third inning. We need to understand the choice as it appeared to the manager: what he had to take as given, and what his options were.

Focus on Points of Choice

In the chapters that follow we will look at conflicts through the eyes of different decisionmakers. These may be civilian officials, campaign advisers, or media executives, or they may be guerrillas, political opponents, or voters — anyone in whose action we are interested. We want to understand the kind of decision they make and why they behave the way they do, so that we might influence them more effectively.

A focus on influencing the choice of a decisionmaker reminds us that even the most global changes we can imagine will involve some individual deciding to do a particular thing differently tomorrow morning. By getting into the shoes of somebody facing a decision, we are also likely to be reminded of the importance of nonquantifiable human factors. We do not let deterministic predictions limit the scope of our choice or become self-fulfilling prophecies. We reconcile the reality of constraints with the possibility of choice.

However predetermined and predictable international relations may look from the outside, that is not how it feels to those who are playing the game. The choices we make may be determined by heredity and environment, but when we get to the office in the morning we cannot say, "Heredity and environment, tell me what to do. Should I sign this piece of paper?" Each of us has the experience of facing choices, reaching conclusions, and acting on them; and once enacted, our decisions can change the course of lives. In the international sphere, it could be said that the United States organized the Bay of Pigs invasion of Cuba in 1961 "because of" historical forces, but from President Kennedy's point of view, *he* decided. To be sure, for each of us many things have to be taken as given. But even if the world is determined in the sense that there is a cause for every event, it is also determined that we must make decisions and act as if we have free will.

Law students study choices; they look at the facts and the law as they appeared to a judge who had to make a decision at a fixed point in time. Although the international system is not as rigidly structured as a legal system, one can study international relations much as one studies law, taking the facts as given but the decision as open. Students of law do not try to guess how a particular judge, with his or her personal idiosyncrasies, would decide the case. Rather they consider how a judge — any judge — in that position and faced with that choice *ought* to decide that case. What would be a sound way for a judge to analyze such a dispute? How would we, as experts, advise a judge faced with that choice to decide? Through such a process we develop our own ability to reach wise decisions.

Be Purposive, Not Reactive

It is most unlikely that we will end up where we want to be unless we have both thought about where that is and directed our actions toward getting there. The quality of advice is measured by how well it furthers some specific purpose. If we are to generate good advice, we will need to have an end in view.

This fairly basic insight was ignored in the spring of 1979, when the United States Senate chose to engage directly in a bit of foreign relations. It unanimously adopted a resolution condemning the postrevolutionary government of Iran for the more than two hundred executions conducted by that government in the previous weeks. Following the overthrow of the Shah, there was uncertainty and confusion over the conflicting authority of the religious leader Ayatollah Ruhollah Khomeini, the cabinet in Teheran, and various revolutionary groups and leaders. During this period, courts were set up in Iran, those charged with having committed political crimes against the people under the Shah were tried, and scores were executed. The U.S. Senate responded to the executions by adopting this resolution. Why?

The question "Why?" asks either for a cause or for a purpose. When two children are in a fistfight, the adult who breaks them up may ask "why" they were hitting each other. The most likely response is something along the lines of "because he hit me first." But that response explains only the cause of the fight, not its purpose. It does not explain what the fighting was supposed to accomplish. An appropriate answer to the question "Why?" can begin with either "Because" or "In order to." The answer can either explain the event as a result of something that happened in the past, or it can explain the event as an act intended to achieve something in the future.

It implies no affection for the revolutionary government of Iran to say that we have a better chance of accomplishing an objective if we act in a way that is forward-looking than if we react to a stimulus that provokes us. Of course, this means knowing what our purposes *are*. In June of 1979, what were the objectives of the United States in Iran? The United States government, which had provided the recently overthrown Shah with extensive military and other support, was politically unpopular in Iran. It was arguably in the interest of the United States to establish some kind of working relationship with the new government of Iran and to avoid driving that government toward the Soviet Union. Presumably, a U.S. goal was to develop patterns of cooperation with the new Iranian government that would deal with practical problems and would avoid the kind of political confrontation that would fuel anti-American feeling. Certainly, in the years immediately preceding the Shah's overthrow, the United States had avoided confronting the Shah over the thousands of political prisoners that were detained during his regime or over killings by his secret police.

Given this situation, it is difficult to believe that any of the one hundred U.S. Senators could have concluded, after five minutes of thought, that a good way to further the interests of the United States would be for the Senate (which had never condemned the Shah) immediately to condemn the new government of Iran for executing people, many of whom had been engaged in torturing and killing political prisoners under the Shah. However unjustified the Iranian executions may have been, the Senate Resolution condemning the executions in Iran was *reactive* — a response to those executions — and not *purposive* — a forward-looking act thoughtfully designed to further some interest or concern. To the extent that it may have had some future-oriented purpose, it was not well-designed to achieve it: Within forty-eight hours the largest anti-American demonstration ever held in the Middle East was held in Teheran. And the policy of executions continued, strengthened by a desire to demonstrate Iranian independence in the face of U.S. pressure.

Actors on the international scene are frequently not looking where they are going because they are too busy looking back over their shoulders. Like the United States Senate, they fall into the trap of reacting to recent actions by others that are upsetting and that engage the emotions of their constituents.

Often the pace of action and reaction is so swift that all concerned ignore both the original cause and the subsequent chain of events; each simply responds to the latest move by someone else. Israeli bombing raids on Palestinian camps in Southern Lebanon were sometimes explained by the Israeli government as part of a program designed to make the Palestinians more peaceful and less violent, but their strongest rationale was "we do it because they use violence against us" rather than "we do it to advance our own purposes." Similarly, Palestinian guerrilla raids into Israel were hardly the consequence of a rational strategy intended to make Israelis more willing to accept Palestinians as peaceful neighbors.

Choose a Purpose Carefully

Purposes are to be formulated, not found. Framing a problem in a skillful way is often the key to managing it. In clarifying our objectives, we are likely to do better if we formulate a purpose, at least to ourselves, in terms of a direction that we would like to go, rather than in terms of a fixed objective that we "must" reach. Public statements of absolute goals such as "end violence," "unconditional surrender," "abolish hunger," "worldwide equality," and "freedom from fear" can raise people's sights, elicit great efforts, and serve as a valuable political strategy. But we want to be utterly candid with ourselves when privately formulating our goals. The goal, even if ambitious, should be conceivably attainable.

We can frame a purpose based on useful criteria, such as: Are the necessary resources under my control? Whom would I need to persuade in order to achieve my objective? And are these people likely to be persuadable? In 1979–80, President Carter's "Rose Garden Strategy" for responding to the Iranian hostage crisis was to decline to campaign, and to stay in the White House until the hostages were released. In this way he hoped to demonstrate concern and leadership, as well as to advance the overarching goal of securing the release of the hostages. These purposes were impossible to accomplish with the resources at the President's disposal. Carter's purposes depended on people on the Iranian side making a decision which, at the time, they had no incentive to make. By organizing his life around the hostages, the President let himself become a hostage of Iranian decisions.

But Carter could have framed his purpose in a different way. While, of course, retaining an interest in the release of the detained diplomats, he could have formulated his immediate purpose as showing that "the United States will adhere to principle and will not pay blackmail or reward kidnapping." Accomplishing such a purpose was under his own control. He could cite the precedent of the North Korean seizure of the *Pueblo*, where the United States refused to pay any ransom and the crew, after eleven months, was released. Rather than defining a purpose that depended for success on the United States' ability to influence Iran, the President could have defined a purpose that depended for success upon Iran's inability to coerce the United States.

The surest way to guarantee success is to formulate a purpose that we have the ability to achieve on our own. The surest way to guarantee failure is to formulate a purpose (like "the immediate release of the hostages") that people who see themselves as adversaries can easily frustrate.

One Good Purpose: Coping Well with Conflict

Our focus in this book is on generating a wise process for dealing with conflicts, whether international, local, or personal. Generating a wise process is quite different from assessing the comparative merits of plans already on the table, or even generating additional competing plans. This distinction between substance and process is not just a question of semantics. There is a high cost in failing to distinguish between (1) What do I think is the best goal? and (2) How shall you and I best proceed when each of us has different ideas about what ought to happen?

The first problem is one of substance: Our purpose is to achieve some result, whether it be universal literacy or a society in harmony with Islamic law. The second problem is one of process: Our purpose is to deal with our differences efficiently, peacefully, and at minimum cost. Sometimes, as in the broad outlines of the terms on which South Africa is becoming a more inclusive society, the eventual resolution or transformation of a conflict is not particularly radical or surprising — it is something that knowledgeable participants and observers alike could see coming for a long time. In cases like these, it makes sense to devote our resources to reaching this next stage with a minimum of pain and expense. Fresh ideas can help with this difficulty, and a substantial portion of our discussion is devoted to how to design a problem-solving process that promotes new thinking on longstanding problems.

Lower transaction costs are a major benefit of increased attention to process. During the height of the Cold War, the United States and the Soviet Union had tens of thousands of nuclear weapons pointed at each other's major industrial and population centers, while our respective economies bankrupted themselves to make yet more weapons. Since each side had enough hardware to blow up the earth several times over, an improved process would, at a minimum, have meant that we all could have been equally insecure at a much lower cost.

This book sets out a blueprint for improving the process of coping with conflict. Experience suggests that the ideas in this book can help anyone manage a tough dispute, get it "unstuck," break it into smaller pieces, and tackle each piece in a constructive way. We present a variety of charts to clarify thinking about different aspects of a problem: What's wrong now, what could we do differently that might help, who could take action, and how might we persuade them? We call these charts "tools" not because of their technical complexity — most are just organized common sense — but because of their emphasis on utility. An experienced carpenter has a variety of tools in his toolbox — measuring tape, chalk, drill, level, wood plane, and so forth, depending on what the job requires. If he is driving a nail, he doesn't use a saw. Knowing which tool, or combination of tools, will address which problem is a product of common sense, experience, and intuition. On the other hand, if the only tool you have in your toolbox is a hammer, every problem will begin to look like a nail.

The balance of this book is a tool box for the problem-solver, suggesting some key questions and approaches for bringing common sense and knowledge to bear in crises and conflict situations. We also hope to encourage the capacity and enthusiasm to continue using and improving such skills — and these tools — in light of future experience.

We contend that even the toughest and most complicated conflict can be handled better, either to improve the results for the players or to get the same results at a lower cost. At the same time, we know that it takes a certain innate optimism to tackle the many obstacles to coping more skillfully with conflict. Incorrigible optimists, we believe that it is always possible for one person with a good idea to change the world — a little.

2

Step into
Their Shoes

A U.S. Army colonel, participating during the Vietnam war in a seminar at the State Department's Foreign Service Institute, seriously questioned the desirability of looking at a conflict from the point of view of one's adversaries. He pointed out that to understand how they saw things might cause us to question the merits of what we were doing or proposed to do. "The better we understand their concerns and their ideas," he said, "the greater the chance that we will lose confidence in the rightness of our own cause." Why bother to understand them if we want to defeat them? Take an example at the moral margin: What if we were dealing with Hitler and the Nazis? If we were advising the Allies, would we really want to "understand" where the Nazis were coming from?

Yes. We want to understand how governments and other international actors see things because therein lies *both* the problem and any possible solution. If we and they saw everything the same way, there would be no differences, no disputes, no conflicts, no wars. There would be little need for international agreements. To understand does not mean to reach an accommodation with someone else. By "understand," we mean "comprehend" rather than "agree with." We would like a snapshot of what is inside that person's head. Such a picture is like having a road map of territory we might want to invade — a clearer view of a target, a better appreciation of a mind we would like to change.

People often think that establishing objective facts will resolve a dispute. Each side in a disagreement may contend that the other was at fault in causing an accident, or both may be claiming proprietary rights to an industrial process that one of them is using. Israel and Syria may be fighting over the Golan Heights; Iran and Iraq may be quarreling over who initiated hostilities. In such circumstances, those attempting to resolve the dispute often assume that what they need is more factual data. They measure the skid marks left by the accident or they study the contested industrial process. They examine the geography of the Golan Heights or carefully review military events.

Yet in each situation, the key to the dispute is not objective truth but what is going on in the heads of the parties. Hopes, even if unrealistic, may cause a war. Facts, even if established, may do nothing to reduce a conflict. Both parties may agree that one developed an industrial process and the other is using it but still disagree about who should have the rights to it. The detailed history and geography of the Golan Heights, no matter how carefully documented, is not the stuff with which one puts to rest a tension between national sovereignty and national security. No study of the war between Iraq and Iran will resolve issues of justification and grievance. Objective reality is unlikely either to be the cause of the problem or the source of a solution.

Experience suggests that the two most helpful qualities in dealing well with differences are an ability to be persuasive and an ability to revise our own thinking in the light of fresh insights.

More data — more facts and figures — merely contribute to our ability to be persuasive or to see a problem in a new way. They are not ends in themselves. To be persuasive, we need to understand how others see the world, their motivations, emotions, and aspirations. To see a problem in a new light, we need to analyze it from perspectives other than our own. In each case, our power depends on our ability to put ourselves in other people's shoes and to see the world from their point of view.

We often handle conflict poorly because we are each prisoners of our own thinking. We tend to judge differences, particularly when we think we know best. Understanding differences is hard work. Frequently we don't know how to go about it.

Explore Partisan Perceptions

We all face a complex world. To make sense of it, we develop perceptions that work as a kind of shorthand, a template that we impose on what would otherwise be a welter of chaotic data. When we see a woman holding a child, we perceive that woman as a mother. We are unlikely to ask her about it; we just assume. We question these perceptions only when we recognize disconfirming data; say the woman and the child have different skin color, then we might assume that we were wrong and that they are not mother and child. If these two are then greeted by a man of different skin color than the woman, our perception might change again. And so on.

There is a Russian saying that everyone looks at the world from the belltower of his own village. Perceptions differ because our experiences differ, and because we select from among our experiences. Each of us observes different data in part because we are all interested in different things. Depending on our specific perspective, our perceptions vary. Terrorists are seen as freedom-fighters by those who would like to be free. Freedom-fighters are seen as terrorists by those who are terrorized.

Based on our perspective, we also selectively view additional information. We tend to collect evidence that supports our prior views and to dismiss or ignore nonconforming data. This screening process has at least three levels: We selectively remember what we want to; we selectively recall what we remember; and we revise our memories to fit our preferences. The more we become convinced of our views, the more we filter out information that would lead us to question them. In reading a newspaper, each of us is likely to skim many stories while noting one in particular that confirms a prior view: "See that? Just what I expected."

To the extent that our current perceptions are distorted, our future perceptions are likely to become even more so. The more entrenched our partisan perceptions become, the more obvious it is to us that we are right and others are wrong.

While working in South Africa, we had some white officials participate in an exercise that highlights the role of partisan perceptions. They looked at a line-drawing which had embedded in it two equally distinct pictures: an old woman looking down, and a young woman looking away into the distance. Beforehand, we had predisposed half the group to see the old woman and half to see the young woman. This predisposition was effected by showing half of them a distorted line-drawing emphasizing the old woman, while the other half of the group was shown a correspondingly distorted drawing emphasizing the young woman.

When shown the genuinely ambiguous drawing where both pictures are equally plausible, the two dozen officials (with one exception) saw only the version of the picture they had been predisposed to see. Without understanding the other's perceptions, two officials tried to persuade each other that the woman in the picture was old or young — eighty or eighteen. Neither had any success. When the "trick" was explained, one official was simply stunned. "If I could be predisposed in thirty seconds to see an ambiguous picture only one way," he said, "just think what thirty years of seeing the world one way has done to me."

We asked the official who had been trying to persuade his colleague that the woman was eighty, not eighteen, whether it would have been different if he had been negotiating with a black. "Oh," he said, "that would have been much easier. I would simply have dismissed without difficulty anything he said, assuming he was lying or trying to hoodwink me in some way. Here I was talking with a trusted colleague. I was genuinely puzzled as to how he could be so wrong."

The real trick of this exercise is that there is no trick. Thirty seconds of seeing things one way can cause us to see things only that way. A lifetime of seeing things one way predisposes us to see only what we expect to see. This is particularly true for those caught up in a conflict, whether a Catholic student in Northern Ireland, or a Tamil separatist in Sri Lanka, or an Israeli settler in the West Bank.

Coping with conflict means coping with the way people think and feel. In any conflict people think and feel differently from one another, and the issue is not whose perceptions are "true" and whose are "false." To provide us with a foundation for dealing with a conflict, we would like to disaggregate the perceptions on all sides — our own as well as those of others — understand them, and be fully in touch with them. The better we understand the way people see things, the better we will be able to change them. There is no magic formula for acquiring understanding. It takes a little time and effort. The tools and techniques suggested here have tended to make the task easier.

In a conflict situation, particularly if it has involved violence, feelings are likely to be more important than thoughts. Participants in a dispute are more apt to be ready for battle than for cooperatively working together on a common problem. Those of us who have seen no more than television reports of the victims of the violence in what was once Yugoslavia can well understand the resulting anger that led to further violence and further anger. A Macedonian officer from the Yugoslav army who had deserted his tank unit explained to a journalist why a federal Yugoslavia was no longer worth fighting for:

> Serbs and Croats in eastern Slavonia can never live together because too much blood has been spilt and the Serbs will never let go of any of this territory. As far as I could work out, the Croats had provoked a lot of the nastiness in the first place but searching for the one who started it is a waste of time. Once it started the massacres were unstoppable. It will never end whether they have a ceasefire, peacekeeping troops or whatever. This is not a war, this is extermination.*

Angry people often fail to hear what others have to say. And whatever they hear, they are likely to put the worst possible interpretation on both the words and actions of someone who is seen as an adversary. If we want to affect what is going on in the heads of others, we will want to be aware of emotions and motivations that may be surging through their hearts. Especially when we are communicating by letter, cable, fax, or telephone, we may be so concerned with ourselves or with substantive ideas that we ignore feelings on their part — feelings that are likely to drown out rational arguments.

Each party to a conflict is certain to have a different estimate of what issues are most important and to have different percep-

*Misha Glenny, *The Fall of Yugoslavia: The Third Balkan War* (New York: Penguin Books, 1992), pp. 125–126.

tions of the relevant history, current facts, his own grievances, and the goals and intentions of all parties to the conflict. Whether we ourselves are a party to a conflict or whether we are dealing with a conflict between two other parties, we can at an early stage illuminate and contrast differing perceptions in a simple and dramatic form.

Chart 1 illustrates one method for doing this. It contrasts in parallel columns one party's perceptions of the issues in a conflict with the perceptions of an opposing party. The example listed, contrasting Syrian and Israeli perceptions of the prospects for peace between those two countries, was prepared in 1975 by a third party putting himself in the shoes of each side in turn and making his best estimate of what people on that side might say. The draft was then refined by reviewing with Syrians and Israelis separately the accuracy of the statements of their own perceptions before showing them the contrasting perceptions of some of those on the other side. This chart, like others in this book, is a tool in our toolbox of approaches to problem-solving.

Chart 1 is reproduced as written approximately twenty years ago. What is striking is how many of the perceptions at that time are still relevant. An up-to-date comparison of partisan perceptions would certainly omit some of those then listed and include some currently more prominent perceptions such as, perhaps, the following:

Syrian perception	Israeli perception
Before we can promise "full peace" or explain what that would mean, we must know that our sovereignty over the entire Golan will be restored.	Before we can agree to return any of the Golan to Syrian sovereignty, Syria must promise full peace and explain what that would mean.

Speaking in another's voice — or writing out perceptions from that person's point of view — accomplishes two tasks at once. It helps free us from our own partisan perceptions. It also helps us

1. Partisan Perceptions

Case: The Syrian and Israeli Conflict, 1975

Some Syrian perceptions

Syria is an underdeveloped country that wants and needs peace.

The Golan is part of Syria and must be returned; if Israel wants us to respect its sovereignty, it must respect ours.

Israel's building civilian settlements in the Golan demonstrates that Israel's true goal is expansion.

If the United States did not give military aid to Israel, it would have to withdraw from Arab land and make peace with the Arabs.

Our interest in peace is demonstrated by our acceptance of the disengagement agreement and the U.N. resolutions and by our resuming diplomatic relations with Israel's strongest ally, the United States . . . The next move toward peace is up to Israel.

In exchange for the Golan (and something for the Palestinians) we could live in peace with Israel.

Israel has no real interest in peace, as demonstrated by its massive military preparations.

We will fight, if necessary, to regain the Golan, which is part of our country.

Israel is keeping the Golan, and therefore we must prepare for war.

Some Israeli perceptions

Syria is a military dictatorship that regularly engages in human rights abuses.

The Golan is not the issue; Syria shelled Israel when Syria held the Golan before 1967.

Syria's insistence on the "rights" of the Palestinians demonstrates that Syria's true goal is to undermine and destroy Israel.

If the Soviet Union did not give military aid to Syria, it would have to accept the existence of Israel and make peace with it.

Our interest in peace is well known, and is further demonstrated by the one-sided disengagement agreement where in exchange for a few words we withdrew from substantial territory . . . The next move toward peace is up to Syria.

In exchange for real peace, we could return to Syria all or most of the Golan.

Syria has no real interest in peace, as demonstrated by its massive military preparations.

It would be absurd for us to give up the Golan without real peace.

Syria is preparing for war, and therefore we must keep the Golan.

see how the perceptions of others, while seemingly intractable, may contain some seeds of flexibility.

When we prepare such a chart we face an initial question: Whose perceptions are we seeking to estimate? Governments and other international actors do not have a monolithic perspective. In many cases there will be a wide range of perceptions. The most direct approach is to focus on the perceptions of those whose minds we are trying to change. Within a government this may be the top leadership; it may be those within the leadership group who appear to be open to changing their minds. Or it may be useful to think of some particular member of a cabinet or government group, either real or hypothetical, who would have to be convinced if that government were ever going to decide as we would like. Considering the risks facing an individual (such as: "If I do that, I may lose my job") can help illuminate the constraints under which a decisionmaker is operating. (In Chapters 4 and 5 we take up the problem of overcoming constraints on our own side that may result from the views of colleagues or constituents and from multiple layers of decisionmaking.)

If we are going to take the time to create a list of perceptions, we want to try to make sure we are getting at what is really on the minds of the parties to the dispute, and not at what we think should be on their minds. It is useful to phrase the perceptions in the voice of the person we are trying to understand, in a form which he or she would find acceptable and which we find plausible and illuminating. People almost always see their own perceptions as legitimate. This does not mean writing a point in precisely the way they might express it. For example, a Palestinian might say, "Israelis are Zionists, and Zionists are racists." Yet we are likely better to appreciate Palestinian concerns if we wrote as a Palestinian perception: "By excluding many of us from the country of our birth, Israel discriminates on racial grounds in favor of Jews and against Arabs." We may or may not agree with such a statement, but it does more to illuminate Palestinian concerns than name-calling statements about Israelis.

In general, it is more useful to draft statements that describe feelings and the impact of what others do than to draft statements that judge or describe others. Understanding the perception of Palestinians that Israel discriminates against Arabs will help us understand why Palestinians judge Zionists to be racists, even if we do not agree with either the perception or the judgment.

We can gain an additional understanding of conflict situations, even those as often discussed as the Cuban missile crisis of 1962, by adding to our best estimate of the partisan perceptions held by each side selectively filtered data that supported those perceptions. Chart 2 uses the Cuban missile crisis to illustrate one organized way of presenting such perceptions and supporting data.

Learning about the perceptions of the leaders of another country is purely an information-gathering operation. We are not at this stage engaging in any policy judgment. We simply want to estimate, as best we can, how other people see things. We assemble information that appears relevant. What is important to them and what is not? We can never be exactly right, and we can never know for sure how accurate we are, but the estimate is worth the effort. We look for their perceptions in what they have written, in what has been written about them, and in what they say. We also engage in role-playing: If we were in their shoes, and these events had happened, how might we see things? Why might they be saying the things they are saying? How would they have to be thinking and feeling for them to make sense of what they are saying and doing?

In some circumstances it is possible to show our draft to the very people whose perceptions we are trying to understand. This is a useful exercise for demonstrating that we have been listening and do understand their point of view. It is also more likely to elicit information about unappreciated interests than a direct interrogation. Before attempting to communicate our own view of a problem to someone with whom we are in disagreement, it is often wise to go through his concerns and arguments first, and to convey our comprehension of them.

In 1983 we showed Stanislov Gavrilov, a Soviet official in Afghanistan, a draft work sheet on Soviet perceptions about the conflict there, phrased from the Soviet perspective. If Soviet forces were to withdraw from Afghanistan, we wrote, "It would be a humiliating defeat; we, the Soviets, would look weak; we could expect a hostile government as our neighbor; perhaps there would be a CIA base there; but the political embarrassment would stop."

"This is a good list," he said, "but you did not mention the typhoid. We have lost many men through typhoid. And you left out the Soviet Navy. They are unhappy that this Afghanistan war is diverting funds from the navy to the army and the air force." We worked together on improving the draft. When it was finished to his satisfaction, he felt that he was dealing with someone who understood Soviet concerns.

In face-to-face negotiations, such a process lays a foundation of credibility. If we can correctly report the perceptions of our adversaries, they may think that perhaps we are also correctly reporting our own. Demonstrating that we understand their point of view may allow them to move beyond defending it, freeing them to listen more openly to our concerns and our arguments. Whether or not it has this effect, we ourselves benefit from better understanding their thinking.

2. Putting Ourselves in Their Shoes

Case: The 1962 Cuban Missile Crisis

Five points the Soviets see as central to the conflict	How the U.S. perceives the points in the left-hand column
The USSR has an unquestionable legal right to put nuclear missiles in Cuba.	Whatever the legal technicalities, nuclear missiles in Cuba are a gross violation of the modus vivendi.
The sovereign Cuban government invited the USSR to do so.	Castro is a Soviet puppet.
It is militarily and politically fair since the United States has missiles in Turkey.	We have already decided to take our missiles out of Turkey.
The United States attacked Cuba at the Bay of Pigs in 1961.	The Bay of Pigs is wholly irrelevant.
The USSR needs to demonstrate that it can and will protect socialist states from imperialist invasion.	The USSR is not in Cuba for defensive purposes.

How the Soviets perceive themselves	How the U.S. perceives the Soviets
The USSR is the sovereign equal of the United States.	The USSR is an aggressive communist interloper in the Western Hemisphere.
Socialist revolutions are the wave of the future, and the USSR supports them.	The USSR promotes socialist revolution wherever it can.
The USSR is the defender of socialist states.	With a nuclear missile base in the Caribbean, the USSR would be a military and political threat to the whole hemisphere.

How the Soviets perceive the U.S.

The United States is arrogant and needs to be taught that the USSR can do what the United States does.

The United States is trigger-happy and quick to use illegal force.

The United States is likely to invade Cuba and oust the Castro regime unless the USSR defends it.

How the U.S. perceives itself

We have military force only for defensive purposes.

We will never back down to communist threats.

We have no intention of invading Cuba.

How the USSR perceives the points in the right-hand column

The USSR has long been vulnerable to U.S. missiles.

Missiles in Cuba simply accelerate the inevitable. Within a very few years our subs and ICBMs will be able to destroy the United States if we should ever have to.

It will be extremely dangerous for the United States to provoke a crisis.

Additional points that the U.S. sees as central to the conflict

A Soviet missile capability in Cuba would let the USSR destroy most of the United States whenever it wanted to.

It would constitute a radical and conspicuous change in the balance of power.

The only time to deal with it is before it becomes operational.

A structured way of exploring partisan perceptions is particularly useful for those directly involved in a conflict. Perceptions are often abstract and unspecific. It is helpful to break them down into more manageable pieces.

Observe from Different Points of View

To understand a conflict in which we are a party, we will want to observe it from at least three points of view. First, we want to be aware of ourselves (Are we angry? losing control? reacting? drifting?) and to consider the conflict from our own point of view (What are our goals? What are our interests? What risks do we see? and so forth). Our point of view is an important starting point. It is, however, only a starting point.

We will also want to observe the situation from the point of view of the other parties to this conflict. Putting ourselves hypothetically in their shoes, what would we see? How does everything look from that vantage point? If we were there, what would be our goals, our interests, our concerns? Would we feel justifiably angry? How does the conflict look from there?

And finally, to gain a more balanced view, how would the situation look from the point of view of a neutral third party? How would a "fly on the wall" describe things? How are the parties behaving? Do they seem to be quarreling, debating, scoring points, bickering, and attacking each other, or are they jointly attacking the problem? Are they wasting time or using it well?

To understand a conflict well we want to observe it from all three positions. (If there are several parties to a conflict, we will want to understand how each sees it.) One who is skilled at dealing with conflict is likely to be adept at jumping back and forth, observing what is going on from each of these three positions, even "on line," while participating in a discussion. The tools for conflict analysis in this book are designed to help provide the perspective that comes from viewing a conflict from different points of view. The most illuminating point of view is likely to be from the second position — seeing the other side of the conflict by standing in the shoes of the person whose mind

3. Three Positions for Observing a Conflict

First Position (Mine): How I see the problem, from my own perspective.

Second Position (Theirs): How I see the problem when I stand in the shoes of the other party to the dispute.

Third Position ("Fly on the Wall"): How a neutral third party would assess the conflict.

These three distinct points of view illuminate a variety of dimensions of a conflict.

we are trying to change. In this chapter and the next, particular attention is devoted to ways of understanding how things look to those we want to influence.

To Gain Empathy, Reverse Roles

Understanding is not simply an intellectual activity. Feeling empathetically how others may feel can be as important as thinking clearly about how others may think.

There is a lot of truth in the old saying that "where you stand depends upon where you sit." Another way of trying to understand the other side's perceptions is literally to sit in a different chair, pretend to be someone on the other side, and try to see the situation from that vantage point.

The chairman of a company held liable for a patent infringement had called in a consultant to advise about the negotiation of a possible settlement on the dollar amount of damages. The case had been in litigation for years. The chairman had been told that if the worst happened, and he should be held liable, he could always settle — but he had little appreciation of how much the other side would expect.

Encouraged by the consultant, the executive agreed to switch seats, moving from his own chair to a chair the consultant had designated as that of the president of the plaintiff company. While the executive initially resisted "playing games," he was eventually persuaded to assume the role of that president and to state the plaintiff's case in the first person as forcefully as he could. Within a few minutes he was playing the role well. Asked how much he might accept in settlement (an amount that, in real life, would be paid out by this executive's own company), he replied (still in his role as the opposing company's president), "Why, I wouldn't take their whole damn company!" Shaken by this experience, and with new insight into what might be required to settle this case, his company raised its settlement offer by one hundred fold. It was rejected, and the judgment was ultimately for even more. An earlier attempt to appreciate the other side's partisan perceptions would no doubt have led him to pursue a wiser strategy from the outset.

Engaging in role reversal is an excellent way to prepare for any situation where our task is to change someone else's mind. Lawyers often prepare for an argument in court by having a friend or colleague pretend to be the absent party — the judge who will hear the case. Such preparation will be even more effective if the lawyer sits in the judge's chair, pretends to be the judge, and from the judge's point of view hears the lawyer's own prepared arguments being delivered by a colleague.

To gain insight by reversing roles, we first identify the person whom we expect to be attempting to persuade (the "absent party") and find a friend or colleague to help us. Our helper is someone who either already knows our side of the conflict or will quickly learn the points we currently plan to make. Then we sit in the chair labeled "absent party," and with the assistance of the helper, come to think of ourselves as being that person. Finally, our helper sits in our chair, assumes our role, and presents our side of the case. While playing the part of someone on the other side of a conflict, we hear our own arguments come back at us. Through such role reversal we can often gain insight and empathy for the other side — sometimes dramatically so — in a way that helps us tailor our arguments to make them more persuasive.

Our purpose in managing conflict cannot be to end all differences. Each party will always see its own reality — each will have strong partisan perceptions about the conflict and his or her role in it. A more useful question than "Who is right?" is: "Given these strong partisan perceptions, how can we move forward?" We need to find a way to cope with conflict despite the fact that people have differences.

Look Behind Statements for Underlying Interests

Role reversal and the other techniques discussed above not only help us understand another's point of view, they help us find room for maneuver by illuminating needs and concerns that lie below the surface.

In a typical conflict, one party makes public statements about its positions, describing what it will and will not do. Other parties make comparable statements about what they will do, what they will never do, and what they insist the first party must do. All sides make demands. Such positions are not only inconsistent with one another but often appear intractable. There is a natural tendency to concentrate on these stated positions since they are the outward symptoms of a dispute. But to concentrate on another party's position may simply cause that position to harden. The more that a position is worked out in detail and the more often it is repeated, the more committed to it a party becomes. Focusing on the other side's position is likely to structure a situation as a contest of will in which an objective becomes not to budge.

Furthermore, a wise outcome is not determined by how much

the parties can be persuaded to compromise on their positions, but rather by the extent to which the outcome takes care of the underlying interests of the parties. Many people become so locked into a position that they forget the very interests that led them to take that position in the first place. They overlook the fact that those interests can often be met in other ways. An employee inventor may claim intellectual property rights in a company's new product. The company, imagining its research and development investment threatened by competition, may deny that the employee has any rights at all. Insisting on the extreme positions staked out by the parties is almost certain to escalate the conflict. A mediator looking behind those positions for the underlying interests could probably find a way to provide the employee with both recognition and fair compensation and at the same time provide the company with the benefits of patent protection.

In taking positions, we tend to assume that an adversary's interests and ours are directly opposed. For instance, if we care about security, we will often assume that others want to harm us. If we care most about sovereignty, we may assume that others want to push us around. From 1979 until 1990, the Sandinista government in Nicaragua challenged North American policies in Central America more directly than any other government in the region before or since. While the U.S. government lobbied for aid to the contras by drawing dire scenarios of a communist beachhead in the Western hemisphere, the Sandinistas' agenda was driven to a much greater extent by their insistence on being treated fairly, equally, and with the dignity befitting a sovereign nation. As the Sandinista Foreign Minister, Father Miguel D'Escoto, put it:

For so long, the United States was like the big *patrone* who came to visit the *campesinos* living on his land. He would come into your house, put his feet up on your table, and all the *campesinos* would line up with their hats in their hands and ask him to fix their problems. Well, now it's *our* house. And the former boss needs to take off his hat when he comes inside to talk to us, and maybe then we can sit at the table together.

After twenty-plus years of occupation by U.S. Marines (1911–1933), and then decades of repressive policies by the U.S.-backed Somoza dynasty (1924–1979), Sandinista officials wanted their government to be treated with respect. But neither the American interest in security nor the Nicaraguan interest in dignity was particularly well-met by the position each side had staked out by 1984: no talks — no direct communication of any kind.

In order to serve our own interests and to maximize the chances for a peaceful and orderly accommodation, we want to preserve some flexibility in the options we propose. This flexibility will enable us to craft options that meet a broader number of our underlying interests — and theirs as well.

The risks of a single-minded pursuit of a specific substantive position are well-illustrated by the breakdown of the 1962 talks under President Kennedy for a comprehensive ban on nuclear testing. A critical question arose: How many on-site inspections per year should the Soviet Union and the United States be permitted to make within each other's territory to investigate suspicious seismic events? The United States proposed that each side be permitted to make at least ten inspections. The Soviet Union offered three. And there the talks broke down, even though no one had made a rigorous attempt to define just what an "inspection" meant — whether it would involve one person looking around for one day, or a hundred people for a month. The parties had not devoted their efforts to designing an inspection procedure that would reconcile the United States' interest in verification with the desire of both countries for minimal intrusion. But the staked-out positions of "at least ten" and "no more than three" became frozen, making it impossible to work with the underlying interests.

In looking behind the other side's positions, we will first be looking for interests which we and they may share. Both passengers in a lifeboat want to get to shore and may subordinate their differences in pursuit of that common purpose. But we will also be looking for areas where their interests differ from ours. Upon examining their respective interests, passengers in a lifeboat may discover that one prefers bread and one prefers cheese, leading to a prompt and amicable division of the rations.

Sometimes, different perceptions and priorities can serve to "make the pie larger" for all concerned; indeed it may actually be easier to reach an efficient settlement where the parties see things differently. If an owner of shares of stock thinks the stock market is high (and is likely to go down) and a potential customer thinks that the market is low (and is likely to go up), no broker who wants to promote agreement will seek to have the two parties agree on the market forecast. The potential for a deal lies in their different perceptions of the present and their different expectations of what will happen in the future.

At the United Nations' Law of the Sea Conference, where negotiations stretched from 1970 to 1982, many developing countries were keenly interested in the issue of technology exchange. They hoped they would be able to acquire from countries that were highly industrialized the advanced technical knowledge and equipment they wanted for deep-sea-bed mining. The United States and other industrialized countries foresaw little difficulty in meeting this desire. They therefore concluded that the subject of technology transfer was unimportant compared with such issues as free passage through straits and the width of the territorial sea. However, by devoting substantial time to working out practical arrangements for transferring technology, they could have made their offer to do so far more credible and far more attractive to the developing countries. By dismissing the subject as a trivial issue to be dealt with later, the industrialized states gave up an opportunity to provide developing countries, at low cost to themselves, with concrete achievement and a real incentive to reach agreement on other issues.

One way to contrast such differing priorities is to write out in parallel columns statements of positions that identify the dispute. These phrases record what each side is actually saying. Then, looking first at their side and next at our own, we can write out phrases that suggest underlying reasons for our different positions. If people on the other side were asked to explain why they took their position, what might they say? How would they justify it in terms of their needs or concerns? There will almost certainly be some shared interests on which it may be possible to build. There will also almost certainly be features of a conflict where we can satisfy some interest of the other side without causing damage to any significant interest of our own. In every situation, some people care more about something; other people care more about something else. Even where both parties care about the same kind of interest — such as prestige or reputation — it may be possible to satisfy both. It might be useful to have a category of "shared interests." For some conflicts, reconcilable interests might best be illuminated by listing separately long-term interests and short-term interests.

In recent years conflicts between Hindus and Sikhs in India have been heating up and capturing headlines with dramatic examples of intolerance and violence. The positions of the two sides are in direct conflict. Yet by studying their underlying interests, one can begin to see possible ways of reconciling them, as Chart 4 illustrates.

4. Positions and Interests

Case: Sikh and Hindu Conflict

Sikhs	Hindus

Positions

Sikhs require an independent nation.	India must remain unified.
Sikhs in the Punjab need a larger percentage of the river and canal waters.	River and canal waters must be distributed equally.

Interests

Substantive interests

Political representation, local control, and prosperity for farms.

Protection from both additional terrorism by Sikh extremists and atrocities committed by Hindus in ethnic clashes.

Ability to practice Sikh religion in peace.

Substantive interests

Continued availability of the Punjab and its agricultural capabilities to India.

Reduction in the likelihood of continued Sikh terrorism and in ethnic and religious clashes in the Punjab.

Symbolic interests and interests in precedent

Protection of minority Sikh rights.

Hindu apology for past violence.

Symbolic interests and interests in precedent

Regain the appearance of Indian unity as unbreakable.

Sikh apology for past violence.

Domestic political interests

Sikhs regain confidence in the Indian government.

Domestic political interests

Sikhs regain confidence in the Indian government.

Finally, the Colonel mentioned at the beginning of this chapter who did not want to understand the other side *did* have a point. The more we learn about the concerns of others, the more likely we are to change our own minds or revise our thinking. We may in fact conclude that the cause for which we have been pressing is misconceived or that we have been misguided. Rethinking our policy is, however, a benefit rather than a cost of understanding an adversary's point of view. Arguably, it would have been a good idea if U.S. decisionmakers had spent more time fundamentally rethinking the ends and means of U.S. action in Vietnam — we might well have been able to reduce the area of conflict and increase the chance of advancing our newly enlightened self-interest.

Understanding how others view a conflict is knowledge that gives us strength. It enhances our ability to influence them. Through exploring the emotions and motivations leading up to a conflict, we can increase our understanding of where their perceptions come from. We can appreciate the basis for their positions and judgments. Becoming aware of the interests that lie behind their positions can focus our attention on the possibility of meeting some of those interests. Such awareness can also give us insight into where there may be room for accord.

3

Focus on
Their Choice

In an international conflict, we are rarely, if ever, writing on a clean slate. Every dispute has a history; we have been sending messages to them and they have been sending messages to us, even if only by silence or by a professed refusal to negotiate. Positions have been staked out. Proposals have been made and rejected. One thing we know for sure: If the conflict is continuing, whatever we have been saying and doing so far *has not worked.* It has not produced the result we want, or we would have turned our attention to other matters by now.

If we are to exert influence more successfully tomorrow, it helps to have today's starting point clearly in mind. We would like to have some useful ways of capturing the interactions between us to date, ways that integrate relevant events and important economic, legal, and other considerations. We propose two such ways, each of which puts us into the shoes of the other party. The first is to analyze past events in terms of the message we have been sending, as it has been received by the other side. The second is to analyze the resulting choice that the other decisionmakers have seen themselves as facing. Together, these two techniques help explain why other parties are doing what they are doing, and point toward what will be needed to overcome barriers to progress.

Understand the Message as They Hear It

When we are involved in a conflict, we are always sending a message to the other party suggesting, implicitly or explicitly, that there is something else they ought to be doing. That suggestion is sometimes conveyed by a threat or warning of possible consequences if they do not do a particular thing, or by an offer or prediction of different consequences if the desired action is taken.

A useful way of figuring out what this message looks like to another party in the dispute is to examine three basic elements of our communication. As of this moment, what is the net effect of everything we have said and done (or not said and not done) in terms of:

- **A demand:** What they hear us asking for;
- **A threat:** What they hear us threatening if our demand is not met; and
- **An offer:** What they hear us offering if they meet our demand.

What we call the demand is what we want them to do in the future. Often we spend our time complaining about the past and leaving it highly uncertain just who it is that we want to do something, and just what it is that they are supposed to do. Our request for action (often unstated) also involves elements of timing (When is it supposed to be done?) and legitimacy (What makes our request reasonable or fair?).

What we call the threat is the consequence to the other side of not doing as we would like — an action we will deliberately take that may make them unhappy. Sometimes instead of a threat, perhaps what we have been sending is a warning of events beyond our control that could result from their failure to take appropriate action. In either case, whether we have been sending a threat or a warning, the effectiveness of this part of the message not only depends upon its content (What are the consequences? When will they occur? Who will impose them? And what makes them legitimate?) but upon the clarity with which those elements are communicated, their credibility, and their probability.

Similar considerations apply to an offer. The impact of the "good" consequences that we are saying will follow if they do take the desired action depends upon answers to the same set of subsidiary questions: Who? When? What? And why are those consequences legitimate?

A good starting point for considering the message we ought to send in the future is to write out the (presumably ineffective) message that we are currently sending. Chart 5 offers a comprehensive list of elements, not all of which will be significant in every case. But the fact that on some points nothing has been said may often be more important than things that were said.

During the bombing of North Vietnam by the United States, the U.S. government was sending a message to the government in Hanoi. The North Vietnamese had been transporting goods along the Ho Chi Minh Trail to supply the antigovernment partisans in the South, the Viet Cong. The United States began a bombing campaign of North Vietnamese positions along the Trail and elsewhere in order to induce the North Vietnamese to stop this supply operation.

It was never clear to North Vietnam exactly what they had to do in order to have the bombing stop. Of course, they knew that if they unconditionally surrendered, stopped all support to anti-

5. Message Analysis

Elements That May Have an Impact

Element		Narrative
Demand	Address	A way of getting the attention
	Addressee	of a particular party
	Tone	with a particular tone of request or demand
	Party or actor	to have the same or another party
	Action	take a desired action
	Time	by a particular time
	Legitimation	for a valid reason.
Threat or warning	Minimum required	If at least a certain action is not taken
	Deadline	by a particular time
	Actor	then some party
	Degree of probability	with some lesser or greater degree of certainty
	Consequences	will take unfavorable action
	Time	by a particular time
	Legitimation	for a valid reason.
Offer or promise	Minimum required	If at least a certain action has been taken
	Deadline	by a particular time
	Actor	then some party
	Degree of probability	with some lesser or greater degree of certainty
	Consequences	will take some favorable action
	Time	by a particular time
	Legitimation	for a valid reason.

6. Contrasting the Message Intended with the Message Sent

Case: U.S. Bombing of North Vietnam

Message element		Message we intended	Message they received
Demand	Address	"Hey! You felt those bombs	"Hey! You felt those bombs
	Addressee	Government of North Vietnam.	tiny weak government of North Vietnam.
	Tone	We insist that	
	Party or actor	you	you must
	Action	stop supplying and encouraging the rebels in the South	stop supporting your comrades and colleagues
	Time	immediately	immediately
	Legitimation	because South Vietnam should be able to determine its own fate."	because we say so."
Threat	Minimum required	"If you don't stop encouraging them	"Unless you cease all forms of support
	Deadline	now	in coming weeks
	Actor	then we	then we
	Degree of probability	will probably	will
	Consequences	bomb you	bomb your civilians
	Time	tomorrow	tomorrow
	Legitimation	to get you to stop."	because we can."
Offer	Minimum required	"If you do stop	"If you do stop
	Deadline	immediately	immediately
	Actor	then we	then we
	Degree of probability	will stop bombing	will consider
	Consequences	and talk with you about the situation	explaining to you
	Time	sometime soon	sometime
	Legitimation	to help establish a government in South Vietnam."	how we are going to set up a puppet government in the South."

government forces in South Vietnam, withdrew all their own forces, cut off supplies, apologized, and offered to pay compensation for damage done, then the United States would almost certainly stop the bombing. But they also knew that all of this was more than the situation required. How *much* more was never adequately communicated.

Some of the things that made the U.S. bombing policy wholly ineffective in influencing the actions of the government of North Vietnam become apparent when one contrasts the message that the United States thought it was sending with the message that was apparently being received, as illustrated by Chart 6. The purely mechanical question of the timing of the desired performance and the consequences of the threat was enough to make the threat unlikely to be effective. In an effort to be reasonable, the United States did not ask for a sudden stopping of all supplies, but rather a gradual tapering off. The result, however, was a message that in substance was: "We will bomb you again tomorrow unless you slow down your supplies over the next few weeks." Since each day they knew they would in any event be bombed the next day, there was no great incentive to stop what they were doing.

After the failure of the bombing message, the U.S. government did not offer North Vietnam the specific terms of a ceasefire in part because of the belief of some government officials that a ceasefire would probably not be accepted. The United States felt, based on North Vietnam's response to the bombing of the Ho Chi Minh Trail, that overtures for settlement had been snubbed. The vicious circle of reenforcing hostility accelerated.

One explanation for the U.S. failure to send a clear message to North Vietnam lies in the internal divisions that then existed among those on "our side" — in particular the government in Saigon, the State Department, and the Department of Defense.

Once President Johnson had ruled out the goal of physically imposing a result on North Vietnam — in part, for fear of getting involved in a land war with China — the purpose of the Vietnam war was to *influence* somebody to make some decision. Yet there was no decision Hanoi could make to stop the war that was more attractive to them than fighting on. The U.S. armed forces could inflict pain, but saw the State Department as responsible for producing the terms of a ceasefire that might be acceptable to both sides. The State Department thought it would be premature and divisive with Saigon to discuss such terms: "When the war has been won, we will be happy to negotiate the terms of the peace." In the long run, as the conclusion of the war bears out, it was easier for the United States to understand and do what Hanoi was clearly demanding — leave — than for Hanoi to understand and do what we were demanding, which was to do enough — whatever that might be — to let us have things our way.

We might have done better in Vietnam to measure the other side's actions against what they were *in fact* hearing, rather than against the message we thought we were sending. Analyzing a conflict in terms of both the message being sent and that being received highlights two key aspects of exerting influence: One is the need to formulate an effective message; the second is the need to transmit that message so that it is accurately received. Each aspect is important. A message is unlikely to be effective if poorly formulated or if not received as intended.

Misunderstanding is all too likely even when parties are face-to-face in the same room. When parties caught up in a conflict are living in different countries, speaking different languages, having their words and deeds edited by the media, transmitted around the world, and summarized in brief headlines, the chance that the message received is the same as the message transmitted approaches zero. The difficult mechanical process of communication is exacerbated by the problem of partisan perceptions and the natural human tendency to put the worst interpretation on what one's adversary says or does. "Assuming the worst" is commonly perceived as a sensible, conservative thing to do. And when dealing with someone seen as an adversary, the worst interpretation is often consistent with our partisan perception. Yet a policy of putting the worst interpretation on what others say will cause us to be mistaken much of the time and to miss many opportunities for reaching agreement.

For example, during the Cuban missile crisis, President Kennedy received a letter from Nikita Khrushchev on Friday, October 26, with a conciliatory tone, and one on Saturday, October 27, with a combative tone. He chose to ignore the second, and, in doing so, avoided making the worst interpretation of his adversary's intentions — and possibly avoided precipitating a nuclear war. It is far better to surmise as accurately as we can what others are really intending to communicate. Thereafter we can weigh the risks of both mistake and deception.

Consider the Other Side's Choice

While message analysis helps us estimate what other players are currently hearing, it is usually insufficient to explain why they are acting the way they are. To pursue that issue, we ask: What is the primary decision those on the other side see themselves as facing? Taking into account not only the message we have been sending but all other factors as well, how do the pros and cons of that decision appear to them? To understand the question to which the other side has been saying no thus far, and to be able to present them later with a more persuasive choice, we again want to analyze the existing situation as it appears to them today. We do this by building on what we know and what we can guess.

Which decisionmaker? Our first task is to identify the person or people our message has been trying to influence. This is usually a leader on the other side whom we have been framing as our adversary, the "enemy," or some other obvious leader in a conflict. This may or may not be the party we choose, after further analysis, to attempt to influence. We might do better to work on someone else. For present purposes, however, we will focus on the individual or small decisionmaking group that people on our side have so far been trying to persuade. For instance, in the 1991 Gulf War, we could single out Saddam Hussein as such a leader.

What decision? The second task is to identify the decision that the party thinks he or she is being asked to make. Typically, there is more than one specific decision being sought, and usually several different ways of formulating each of them. Consider the choice faced by Prime Minister Margaret Thatcher at the time of the Falklands/Malvinas crisis. What did she think she was being asked to say yes to? At various times she might have heard herself being asked to abandon self-determination for the Falkland Islanders, to yield to illegal military force, or to turn the islands over to Argentinean rule.

If we want to understand how a person or small group sees their choice, we will want to imagine how they might respond to the question, "What are they asking you to do?" Usually the person being pressed — for example, Prime Minister Thatcher — will describe what she is being asked to do in simple, if extreme, terms: "They are asking me to give up everything." "They want us to surrender." And when opponents tend to see issues in extreme terms, posing such a simple choice may be the best way to get inside the mind of the target decisionmaker.

What perceived consequences? Having identified both a decisionmaker and the question she faces, we next try to estimate

7. Currently Perceived Choice of a Decisionmaker

General Example

"Shall I now abandon a position that we have taken and make a concession?"

Consequences if I say YES	Consequences if I say NO
− I will be criticized.	+ I maintain popularity.
− I may lose power.	+ I keep power.
− Our side backs down.	+ We stand firm.
− We will have to figure out what concession to make.	+ There is no decision to make.
− Any concession will reduce our bargaining position.	+ We maintain our bargaining leverage.
− We give up the opportunity of getting anything better.	+ We can always make some concession later if we have to.
	+ We keep our options open.
BUT	**BUT**
+ We may improve the chances of obtaining an agreement.	− We may postpone reaching an agreement.

Even this general example can provide a powerful explanation for a deadlock.

the consequences that she anticipates would follow from answering that question yes or no. What would be the expected results of saying yes? What would be the expected results of saying no? Again, it has proved helpful to organize and write down in a chart our estimate of how that choice looks, phrased from the perspective of the party we want to influence.

Chart 7 illustrates a way of appraising the decisionmaker's existing state of mind. It describes the present situation, not what that situation ought to be, and helps us answer the question, "Why are things deadlocked now?" This Currently Perceived Choice (CPC) chart attempts to explain why people on the other side, from their perspective, are reasonably saying no to what they hear us asking them to do. Of course, it is most unlikely that the person faced with a choice has in fact written out such a chart. Nonetheless, we can better understand the difficulties we will have in exerting influence if we make explicit our estimate of the considerations that are important to the person whose mind we hope to change.

Although we are trying to estimate an actual state of affairs, the construction of such a chart is not so much a mechanical act as a creative one. It puts to use our earlier analyses of partisan perceptions, positions, interests, message sent, and message received. If a leader were to say yes to the choice that she believes she is now being asked to make, what future consequences might she expect?

To make a CPC chart, our first task is to phrase the choice as the decisionmaker would see it. Then we generate possible consequences that might be perceived as important by the person at the point of choice. We draft these consequences in simple, clear phrases and select the half-dozen or so most important ones for each side of the choice, placing them in some rough order of importance. One way to generate consequences of possible importance to the decisionmaker is to run through a short checklist of considerations, such as those listed in Chart 8, phrased from the decisionmaker's point of view, that might well be important to *any* leader being asked to make an important decision.

Following this approach, we could highlight, for example, how Iraqi President Saddam Hussein might have perceived his choice in early February 1991 regarding the withdrawal of his troops from Kuwait. Given the choice he thought he was facing, as

8. Consequences Likely to Be Important to a Decisionmaker

For me personally

Will I lose power?
Will I be criticized?
Will I be able to explain and justify the decision easily?
How will it affect my reputation in the press and public?

For my colleagues and supporters

Will they support me?
Will they like the decision?
Will they be hurt by it?

For the larger domestic community

Will the decision be popular?
Will it be good for the community?

Internationally

What will be the military or strategic consequences?
Will allies and friends support the decision?
Will there be broad international political support?

As a matter of policy

Is the decision consistent with what we have been saying?
Is it the right thing to do?
Will it set a good precedent? a bad one?

Other options?

Is this a fading opportunity?
What do we lose by waiting?
Can we make the decision and keep other options open?

This checklist of questions is designed to help us identify consequences that may be important to someone we are trying to influence.

outlined in Chart 9, it is not hard to understand why he was saying no.

Since important decisions are always a balancing act, the decisionmaker is usually weighing the incentives and disincentives for deciding a certain way. Until now, they have been coming down on the side of saying no. In constructing a CPC chart, we should also list some of the decisionmaker's reasons for saying yes, perhaps at the end of a long list of reasons for saying no. Chances are the party has considered at least a few reasons to agree with us but has rejected them.

When we created Saddam Hussein's Currently Perceived Choice chart in February of 1991, in the middle of the Gulf War crisis, we were relying on our own research and materials generally available to the public, such as information published in the *New York Times*. But apparently we had come reasonably close to estimating Hussein's choice as he perceived it. When he met with Yevgeni Primakov, the Director of the Soviet Institute for World Economy and International Relations at the end of October 1990, the two discussed the possible withdrawal of Iraqi forces from Kuwait. Primakov relayed how problematic Saddam Hussein found this possibility.

> Saddam asked, "How can I announce the withdrawal of troops if I am not informed how the question of the removal of U.S. forces from Saudi Arabia will be resolved? Would the U.N. sanctions against Iraq be lifted, or would they remain in force? How would my country's desire for an outlet to the sea be ensured? Would there be some sort of linkage between an Iraqi withdrawal and solution of the Palestine problem?" Without knowing the answer to these questions, he said, he could not relax his position: "For me, that would be suicidal."*

*Michael R. Beschloss and Strobe Talbott, *At the Highest Levels: The Inside Story of the End of the Cold War* (Little, Brown, 1993), p. 279.

9. Currently Perceived Choice

Case: Saddam Hussein, Early February 1991

"Shall I now say I will withdraw from Kuwait?"

Consequences if I say YES	Consequences if I say NO
− The bombing may continue.	+ I stand up to the United States.
− The blockade may continue.	+ I keep my options open for better terms from the U.N.
− I yield to a U.S. ultimatum.	+ I can fight indefinitely and hope to outlast the United States.
− Israel may still attack as retaliation for the Scud missiles.	+ I can always agree later.
− I look weak.	+ I look strong.
− I lose credibility in the Arab world.	+ I am a hero to many Arabs.
− The United States will make new demands such as compensate Kuwait, compensate hostages, destroy Iraqi military, change the regime, accept war crimes trials.	+ I can continue to defy Western will by creating more oil spills and setting the Gulf on fire.
− I may be hanged as a war criminal.	+ Dying a martyr is better than dying a war criminal.
	BUT
	− The war and blockade will continue.

This chart, published in the Boston Globe *on February 8, 1991, was intended to suggest why, from Saddam Hussein's point of view, he was behaving reasonably even after Desert Storm began. The tool is nonjudgmental. It simply asks us to estimate the state of mind of someone we are trying to influence.*

Saddam Hussein still had no answer to those questions in February 1991, as U.N. troops were attacking. And without answers, even warfare against superior forces (with him in charge) looked better to him than committing political suicide.

Focusing on the specific choice of one individual, while it helps clarify our thinking, does obscure differences of opinion within a government and the complex interplay that takes place within a bureaucracy. Sometimes a two-step process is helpful, in which we first list the consequences to the individual of suggesting to his own side that a certain course of action be followed, and then below that list the consequences to the government or to the decisionmakers as a group. Some of the consequences we listed in Chart 9 are ones that President Hussein might think of as personal ("I look weak") and others that he might think of as affecting the government ("The United States will make new demands . . ."). There are no doubt additional ways to illuminate these different kinds of anticipated consequences. As we have noted, decisionmakers themselves rarely sort out their thoughts as precisely as we are trying to do, and we are not looking for mathematical precision. We are thinking as clearly as we can in order to improve our appreciation of a very human choice.

See Changing Their Choice as Our Problem

A CPC chart should explain why someone has not made a particular decision. The other side's perceptions, their assumptions, their interests, and what they hear us saying provide the picture of how the conflict looks from their point of view. Looking separately at each of those aspects gives us some clues on how to proceed. We may want to correct misperceptions, reduce emotions, respond to their interests, or transmit a more effective or more easily understood message than the one they have been receiving.

We wish to influence a person who is currently saying no rather than acting in a manner more to our liking. After we have made a Currently Perceived Choice chart, we may next want to construct a Target Future Choice chart — a tool that will help us formulate a future choice to which that person might agree. Constructing a TFC chart for a decisionmaker is a useful step in turning a problem into a solution. Creating a future choice that is more palatable to our decisionmaker will often be easier than trying to alter the consequences of the current choice — easier than changing the carrot or the stick. To do that might require altering public opinion, the perceptions of colleagues and constituents, or some current international norm. We need to sketch out the parameters of a *new* choice — a choice where the net consequences of saying yes will appear more favorable than those of saying no. Rather than escalating threats or making new offers, we will want to change the content of the question, the process by which it is presented, or both. As with a child's see-saw, the easiest way to change the balance is not to add weight to one side or the other but rather to shift the fulcrum.

When we constructed a Currently Perceived Choice chart, we started with the question the decider probably saw himself as facing and then estimated the consequences he could anticipate. Now, when we construct our Target Future Choice chart, we look ahead a few days, weeks, or months and start with consequences that we want the decider to anticipate. When we know the kind of consequences we want to flow from the new choice, we can work our way back toward inventing a choice that could produce those consequences. What we will not yet know is what the new question will be.

Coming up with that new question will be an exercise in "solving for X" — generating a proposal that is likely to be seen as leading to the kind of consequences we now believe are necessary if our target decisionmaker is to say yes. The hypothetical

10. Target Future Choice of a Decisionmaker

General Example

"Shall I now accept the X Plan?"

Consequences if I say YES

+ My personal standing is secure.

+ I can easily justify the decision to my constituents.

+ I will not be seen as backing down.

+ The action is reasonably consistent with our principles and past statements.

+ It will not set a bad precedent.

+ All things considered, it is a constructive step for dealing with this problem.

+ We still keep many of our future options open.

BUT

− Some hardliners will criticize me.

Consequences if I say NO

− I will be subjected to some criticism.

− The problem will not go away.

− It is likely to get worse.

− I will miss a fading opportunity.

BUT

+ Some hardliners will no doubt support me.

proposal we come up with can be called the X Plan, to emphasize that its component terms are not yet worked out, but that the consequences of accepting it must look more attractive to the other side than the consequences of rejecting it. Chart 10 sets out one format for such an analysis.

For any X Plan to be adopted, all the relevant parties will need to find it desirable. We will need to construct a TFC chart for each player — for our side as well as for theirs. Each TFC chart notes consequences which that side might realistically be expected to foresee if it should say yes or no to the question "Shall I now accept the X Plan?"

Charts 11–14 examine the ongoing conflict between Turkish and Greek Cypriots concerning sovereignty over the island of Cyprus. The first two show the currently perceived choices that the President of Cyprus and the leader of the self-proclaimed Turkish Republic of Northern Cyprus may be facing. Charts 13 and 14 show target future choices as they should perhaps appear in the future if each side were going to respond affirmatively to the question "Shall we now agree to the X Plan for the island of Cyprus?"

If the first two charts accurately capture how the two leaders see their respective choices, then no wonder they have been saying no thus far! If we were to design an X Plan to which they might at some future time say yes, what interests would it have to satisfy? Remember that the terms of any X Plan will need to be the same for both parties.

11. Currently Perceived Choice

Case: President Clerides of Cyprus, June 1993

"Shall I now agree to the recent U.N. proposal as is?"

Consequences if I say YES	Consequences if I say NO
− I may be seen as giving in to Turkish demands without extracting enough concessions from them.	+ Refugees and conservatives will approve; Greek Cypriot political stability is maintained.
− I will lose political power.	+ I maintain control of the government, without bureaucratic reshuffling to incorporate Turkish Cypriots.
− We Greek Cypriots will have to share our economic success with Turkish Cypriots and help them to develop economically; overall economic progress will be slowed down.	
− Agreement will encourage (possibly violent) opposition from rightists who continue to support unification with Greece.	+ I do not jeopardize the economic success Greek Cypriots have achieved since 1974.
	+ I keep economic and international pressure on Turkish Cypriots and the Turks.
− I may be providing a springboard for eventual Turkish takeover of the island if Turkish troops do not withdraw.	+ I keep alive the possibility of a solution that incorporates a more centralized and powerful federal government.
	+ I stand up to Turkish pressure by refusing to succumb to a fait accompli.
	+ I avert formalization of a de facto partition of Cyprus on Turkish terms.
	+ I can always say yes later.

BUT	**BUT**
+ Unification is achieved.	− The U.N. is displeased.

12. Currently Perceived Choice

Case: Turkish Cypriot Leader Rauf Denktash, June 1993

"Shall I now agree to the recent U.N. proposal as is?"

Consequences if I say YES

− We risk political, economic, and cultural domination as well as violence from the Greek Cypriots who support unification with Greece.

− I lose power with my constituents.

− We lose control of our own affairs in exchange for an indeterminate future.

− I lose my own political power when a federal government is set up.

− We lose the backup of Turkish troops, leaving us vulnerable to attack if anything goes wrong.

− Turkish Cypriots who were uprooted in 1974 or earlier lose their property once again.

− Turkey may not agree to withdraw its troops, may undermine our credibility, and may hurt our chances for a lasting resolution.

BUT

+ Unification is achieved.

+ The economic boycott ends.

+ Domination by Turkey in Turkish Cypriot affairs diminishes.

Consequences if I say NO

+ We maintain autonomy and are not dominated by Greek Cypriots.

+ There is no possibility of unification with Greece.

+ Turkish troops maintain pressure on Greek Cypriots.

+ There is little violence since the communities are separated and the UNFCYP peacekeeping force maintains a ceasefire.

+ I can always say yes later.

BUT

− We have to rely on Turkey for our economy.

− Economic boycott and international nonrecognition continues.

13. Target Future Choice

Case: President Clerides of Cyprus

"Shall I now accept the X Plan?"

Consequences if I say YES

+ I retain power and influence.

+ We have a workable timetable for the withdrawal of Turkish troops.

+ We have adequate access to the North.

+ We break the stalemate and avoid more violence.

+ The island will be unified under a central government.

+ A minority of citizens is not so empowered as to freeze the legislative process (as in 1960).

+ Economic growth continues.

+ We gain good press and international favor, leading to more aid and trade.

+ I enact an indigenous Cypriot solution and not one imposed by outsiders.

+ The agreement will leave us better off than we are today.

BUT

− Hardliners are upset, and may be disruptive.

Consequences if I say NO

− I may lose power.

− The stalemate continues.

− Important interests are not addressed.

− We miss out on a fading opportunity.

BUT

+ Hardliners are happy.

14. Target Future Choice

Case: Turkish Cypriot Leader Rauf Denktash

"Shall I now accept the X Plan?"

Consequences if I say YES

+ We will be able to cohabit with the Greek Cypriots and still maintain adequate legislative power and civil rights for our community.

+ I retain power and influence.

+ The island is unified, and relatively autonomous regions are linked by a federal government.

+ We break the stalemate and avoid more violence.

+ Our economic dependence on mainland Turkey ends.

+ Our economic stagnation ends.

+ We gain good press and international favor, leading to more aid and trade.

+ I enact an indigenous Cypriot settlement and not one imposed by outsiders.

+ We show that we are interested in peace and trustworthy in our negotiations.

+ We will be better off than we are today.

BUT

− Hardliners are unhappy.

Consequences if I say NO

− Important issues remain unaddressed.

− I may never get another chance like this; I may lose power.

− The stalemate continues.

− We continue to pursue the "Turkish Republic of Northern Cyprus," which is not a viable long-range option.

BUT

+ Hardliners are happy.

Coping effectively with a conflict means being persuasive to the players on the other side — and on our side. Being persuasive requires us to think clearly about changing how people see their choice. In doing so, we do not want to treat any aspect of that choice as fixed and immutable, be it the decisionmaker, the proposed decision, the elements that influence his or her decision, or perceptions that may effect the weighing of those elements. All are potentially subject to change. As we develop a new plan of action for ourselves, we greatly benefit from having set out the other side's currently perceived choice and important parameters of a preferred future choice.

We are often asked: But what if the other side is *crazy?* It's nice to have a logical analysis, but how does it help when the other side won't listen to reason?

Muammar Quadaffi of Libya was derided as "Quadaffi duck" by one U.S. President; Saddam Hussein's reasoning was described as "like something out of Disneyland" by another. Serb militants fighting on in Bosnia were said to be beyond reason, driven by anger and revenge. Maybe. Name-calling encourages the perception that the other side is stupid, deranged, or malevolent. While ill will (on either side) is often a plausible explanation, stupidity or insanity is *rarely* what is causing a conflict. When we look back on decisions made by Quadaffi, Saddam Hussein, and Serb militants, we may not like what we see; we may not share their values or priorities. But to say that their conduct is irrational excuses our own behavior much too easily.

When we look more carefully at behavior that strikes us as irrational or driven solely by emotion, we often find good reasons for what others are doing. For example, if we look at the choice as it may have appeared to a paramilitary Serb in July of 1993, what would have been the perceived consequences of yielding to the U.N.'s demand for a ceasefire? How would that choice have

15. Currently Perceived Choice

Case: Paramilitary Serb, July 1993

"Shall I now stop fighting in response to the U.N. call for a ceasefire?"

Consequences if I say YES	Consequences if I say NO
− I abandon the cause of Greater Serbia for which many have died.	+ I remain loyal to the Serbian cause
− We gain no more territory.	+ We can gain more territory.
− We will have to yield some territory won in battle.	+ We can probably hold the land we have won.
− Many Muslims may be put back into our villages and towns.	+ We have a good chance of keeping our hard-won territory ethnically clean.
− We admit that foreigners, unwilling to fight, can tell us what to do in our own country.	+ We adhere to the internationally recognized principle of self-determination.
− The U.N. may arrest and try me as a war criminal.	+ There is little chance of a war crimes trial (someone will have to catch me first).
	+ We keep our options open. We can always stop fighting later.
BUT	**BUT**
+ The terrible fighting stops.	− The terrible fighting goes on.

looked? If newspaper accounts are accurate, it may have looked somewhat like that indicated in Chart 15.

The United Nations voted economic sanctions against Iraq as a way of putting pressure on Saddam Hussein to get out of Kuwait. The United States then said that it would maintain the oil blockade whether Saddam Hussein withdrew from Kuwait or not. Pain is not pressure unless there is a way to avoid the pain. Economic sanctions have no more political impact than a drought unless there is a decision that can stop them. By announcing that it would continue the blockade even if Iraq withdrew all its forces from Kuwait, the United States effectively undercut any incentive the U.N. economic sanctions gave Iraq to withdraw from Kuwait. Threatening Serbs with war crimes trials if they were to stop fighting and accept U.N. supervision of a ceasefire, whatever its moral message, certainly reduced any incentive a Serb might have had to accept a ceasefire.

The fact that we see ourselves as behaving reasonably does not mean that others are being unreasonable. In most if not all international conflicts, leaders on each side are reasonably saying no to what they hear others demanding. The key to stepping out of this dilemma is to focus first on the other side's choice, not ours, and to see what we might do to change it. Drawing up a Currently Perceived Choice chart — even where it is only a good guess — can often disclose why a seemingly erratic decisionmaker is choosing a particular course of action. Looking at the other side's choice, and assuming that they will behave rationally, substantially increases the chance that we will.

4

Generate
Fresh Ideas

Italian folklorists tell the story of three workers cutting stones in the hot sun. When the first was asked what he was doing, he replied, "I am chipping these stones to make them just the right size." The second replied, "I am earning my wages." To the same question the third replied: "I am building a cathedral."

It is all too easy to get caught up in a narrow perception of a problem. We are likely to get so enmeshed in the nitty-gritty of coping with a crisis that we lose sight of our objective. Stepping back to look at the big picture is often the best way to figure out where to direct our energies in the resolution of a dispute. Yet to tell someone to stop thinking the way they have been is like telling a child not to think of elephants. To reframe a problem is likely to require both a clear purpose and an action to advance that purpose. To break out of an existing frame and to clarify both purpose and proposed action will require fresh ideas. This chapter suggests a way of coming up with such ideas.

Think Systematically

Time, including preparation time, is precious, especially in the middle of an international crisis. We want to use our time efficiently to examine potential roadblocks to the resolution of the conflict, to figure out which ones may be impeding progress and which of those we may be able to anticipate, evade, or overcome. Our goal is to devise an action plan — a step-by-step agenda of small, discrete steps for attacking a problem.

Often, however, we will start with different ideas at varying levels of generality about what are effectively different problems. How can we go about sorting these ideas out? The tool we describe in the following paragraphs — a Four-Quadrant Analysis — has turned out to be a powerful and basic aid to clear thinking in all kinds of conflict situations. It helps people understand where they agree and where they disagree, it helps multiply good ideas, and it helps people think about whether what they propose makes sense. We often use this tool to structure the brainstorming process, to help us figure out where we are stuck and why, or to analyze a success in the hopes of replicating it.

The analytical thinking involved in dealing with a problem can be sorted into the four categories shown in Chart 16: *What is wrong?* (Quadrant I), *General diagnoses* (Quadrant II), *General approaches* (Quadrant III), and *Action ideas* (Quadrant IV). Busy practitioners, who often feel that they do not have the luxury of analysis, tend to jump from problem to response (from Quadrant I to Quadrant IV), without a cogent theory of why they are doing what they are doing. Academics, in contrast, often theorize about why in general certain problems occur (Quadrant II) and what in general might be done about them (Quadrant III). Looking forward to developing an action plan for a specific conflict, we want to merge the approach of a busy practitioner, who has little time

16. A Four-Quadrant Analysis for Problem-Solving

Quadrant I What is wrong?	Quadrant II General diagnoses	Quadrant III General approaches	Quadrant IV Action ideas
Perceptions of: • disliked symptoms; • a preferred situation; and the gap between them.	Possible reasons why the problem hasn't been resolved or the conflict settled. Possible causes (about which somebody could do something) of the gap in Quadrant I.	Possible strategies for overcoming the identified diagnoses.	Ideas about who might do what tomorrow to put a general approach into action.

for theory, with that of an academic, who may have limited interest in a practical outcome.

A Four-Quadrant Analysis encourages systematic yet creative problem-solving. We participated in this kind of creative session in February 1993, focusing our energies on the process of constitutional negotiations then taking place in South Africa. The parties had been seeking agreements in principle, which they would sell to their constituents, returning later to negotiate the refinement and implementation of those agreements. At the time there was widespread dissatisfaction regarding progress at the negotiating table. Using a Four-Quadrant Analysis of the problem and the strategies that had been tried so far (as described in Chart 17), we concluded that while the process of trying to agree on the major points and filling in the details later is familiar and useful in many circumstances, it was hindering progress in this case. As a result, we proposed that in parallel to the official negotiations,

17. A Four-Quadrant Analysis

Case: Negotiating a New Constitution, South Africa, February 1993

Problem	Diagnosis	Approach	Action plan
Many decisions need to be made. Risk of delay. Rising tide of violence. Political leaders losing control. Need for swift action.	The process of first agreeing in principle, and later on implementation is causing extensive delay. That process is useful when: • there are few parties • few constituents • much trust • parties have worked cooperatively before	Need a process which minimizes delays and works when: • there are many parties • and many public constituents • a low level of trust • parties see each other as adversaries	Stimulate a parallel process: government and ANC, without commitment, start producing a working draft of a comprehensive, operational document that can be enacted when needed.

The analysis suggested that the process then being used (which works well in some situations) should be supplemented by a process that tends to work better between perceived adversaries.

the parties get to work on jointly producing a nonbinding draft of the comprehensive document that they would sooner or later need if any agreement were to be reached and implemented.

A Four-Quadrant Analysis is sufficiently simple to be quickly accepted by diverse members of a group and sufficiently basic to be applicable to almost any situation. It is also useful for multiplying good ideas by allowing participants to go backward and forward from one quadrant to another. If a specific idea (in Quadrant IV) seems promising, what is the general approach (Quadrant III) of which that specific idea is an example? Can we think of other specific ways in which that general approach might be implemented? If a general approach seems sound, what is the diagnosis (Quadrant II) to which that is an appropriate response? Can we think of other ways in which we might respond to that diagnosis? And so forth.

Diagnose Obstacles to Progress

Using this Four-Quadrant Analysis, we can start trying to get a negotiation unstuck by identifying the symptoms of the problem — by asking "What is wrong?" One common symptom is poor choices made with incomplete information under intense time pressure. Another symptom might be burdensome, time-wasting meetings where people's talents are not put to good use. What causes such difficulties during negotiations? Three explanations stand out.

We fail to analyze. When medical doctors are faced with a patient's complaint, they have a systematic way of diagnosing the underlying illness — that is, of looking for a cause of the symptoms. Before prescribing medication, they check temperature, blood pressure, pulse, and breathing, they take a careful history of the patient's previous illnesses, and they listen to his complaints. Most people who deal with conflict, by contrast, have no such organized way of diagnosing a situation before making decisions about what to do. We lack a diagnostic checklist to help us be sure — whether or not we are under pressure of time — that we have gathered the pertinent information we need to make a good decision.

Working alone, we use only one "map" of the world. A map helps us understand the world by simplifying it. A useful subway map of Boston, for example, eliminates curves and distorts distances while highlighting information about stations and transfers for passengers needing to get from one place to another. At the same time, such a map is grossly inaccurate; it would be a dangerous map for someone to use who was digging up the streets or planning a new extension to the subway. To understand a complex system such as a city, we would want to consult an atlas of different maps and integrate the information from each of them.

A significant conflict is like a city in that it is complex and has so many facets that one point of view will never give us the whole picture. Yet when we are working on a problem on our own, we often see things exclusively through the lens of our own partisan perceptions. We fail to explore other points of view that would offer enlightening perspectives.

Working in a group, we are crippled by our group assumptions. Working with others, our thinking is constrained by conventional ways of acting. In diplomatic circles, for instance, protests are often lodged not because they do any good but because protesting is "what is done." Any freely invented option may be pounced upon by adversaries as an official offer, or treated by critics at home as a concession. People at the top of an organization often see their primary concern as having their existing views prevail. Lower-level bureaucrats are likely to accord a cool reception to fresh thinking. Participants in a meeting often operate using unspoken assumptions, such as:

"An idea that I suggest is a proposal that I am recommending."

"My goal is to generate an idea which others will like."

"We are looking for something on which we will all agree."
"My name will be attached to any idea I advance."
"I am going to be judged by the merits of my ideas."
"Bad ideas will reflect poorly on those who suggest them."
"Pointing out flaws in an idea is a valuable activity."

Such assumptions produce heavy self-censorship. Even without these barriers to sharing new ideas, most of us are untrained in the art of generating fresh ones. The imaginative creativity of a typical four-year-old is quashed rather than fostered by years of formal education and socialization. We need ways to break free of these kinds of constraints without turning every meeting into a free-for-all.

Try Some New Approaches to Analysis

If our goal is to develop general approaches for managing the debilitating symptoms of a conflict, an appropriate test of our diagnostic tool is not whether it yields a scientifically exact diagnosis but whether it yields enough useful information to help a practitioner prescribe therapy. One can divide all snakes into those that are shorter than a meter and those that are longer than that. Those categories are scientifically precise — but useless. One can also divide snakes into those that are poisonous and those that are nonpoisonous. That distinction turns out to be less scientifically precise (some snakes are slightly poisonous; others change with age), but far more useful to those who want to deal with snakes. The diagnostic tools we suggest below necessarily divide the world into categories that are not always theoretically pure, but we have found them to be consistently helpful.

Negotiators, like doctors, need a diagnostic checklist. It can help us get our hands around a problem and highlight any gaps in our analysis so far. This checklist does not tell us what the answers to the questions should be. Answers will vary depending on the dispute. Our rule of thumb regarding use of such a checklist is simply this: We will be better off if we make a rigorous attempt to answer each question as part of our preparation than if we do not make the attempt. Applying a structured set of questions concerning the parties and the issues helps us figure out more precisely what is wrong, and makes it more likely that we can develop a focused plan for fixing it.

The checklist we have developed at the Harvard Negotiation Project divides a potential conflict into Seven Elements, with questions under each heading, as presented in Chart 18. Most of these items were originally introduced as a way of explaining the different components of negotiation, but subsequent experience has proven their usefulness as a preparation tool in any situation where persuasiveness may be demanded. By looking behind a position (what the other side demands or asserts) for the underlying interests (the wants, needs, and concerns that cause them to make that demand or assertion), we tend to create more flexibility for ourselves. And while the line we suggest between positions and interests may not always be precise, it turns out to be extremely practical. As with any attempt to make sense of the real world, one must choose between the advantages of a list that is long and those of one that is short.

Interests. Parties often find themselves locked into extreme positions from which they find it nearly impossible to make concessions. Positions, however, have been constructed to meet some underlying need, concern, want, or fear. Unfortunately, they are regularly treated as the *only* way in which a party's interests might be met. Making unstated interests explicit tends to open up other ways to accommodate them.

Often, especially when engaged in hard bargaining, parties

18. Seven Elements of a Conflict Situation

Interests

Have the parties explicitly understood their own interests?
Do the parties understand each other's priorities and constraints?

Options

Are sufficient options being generated?
Is the process of inventing separated from the process of making commitments?

Legitimacy

Have relevant precedents and other outside standards of fairness been considered?
Can principles be found that are persuasive to the other side? To us?

Relationship

What is the ability of the parties to work together?
Is there a working relationship between their negotiators?
Are the parties paying attention to the kind of relationship they want in the future?

Communication

Is the way the parties communicate helping or interfering with their ability to deal constructively with the conflict?
Are mechanisms in place to confirm that what is understood is in fact what was intended?

Commitment

Are potential commitments well-crafted?
Does each party know what it would like the other party to agree to?
If the other side said yes, is it clear who would do what tomorrow morning?

Alternatives

Does each side understand its Best Alternative To Negotiated Agreement — its BATNA?
Are the negative consequences of not settling being used to bring the parties together?

stake out extreme positions that ignore the other side's concerns. A U.S. arms control negotiator was asked in the 1980s whether he could design a plan that the then-Soviet Union could accept. "Sure, that would be easy," he said, "but our side would never agree to it." Asked if he could draft a proposal that would meet both U.S. and Soviet interests, he reacted, "Their interests? Their interests are *their* problem!"

As advisers to this negotiator, we might have wanted to point out that the United States itself had a strong interest in meeting the interests of the Soviet Union, at least enough so that it would both sign and implement an agreement. Meeting Soviet interests, as well as our own, was not "their" problem but one that we shared with them. Every buyer wants the seller to be sufficiently satisfied to enter into the deal. Working out a deal satisfactory to both sides is a joint concern and a joint opportunity.

When reviewing interests, consider asking: Have discussions to date focused on demands and concessions? Are parties being forthcoming about their underlying concerns? Could each answer, for themselves and for other parties to the conflict, what they hope to accomplish, and for what purpose?

Options. When players deal with each other by traditional hard bargaining, they often fail to explore sufficient options. We tend to think of "our" options designed to meet our interests and "their" options designed to meet their interests. Yet the shared goal is to find an option that meets the interests of both sides at least well enough to be acceptable to them.

When thinking about options, we ask ourselves: Are there enough possibilities on the table? Are too few variables — timing, money, risk, precedent, parties — under consideration? If we could use more options, might some new voices help? Should we explore other ways of generating more possible agreements or pieces of an agreement? Most of this chapter is devoted to generating new options, both *substantive* options — fresh ideas for resolving a dispute — and *process* options — ideas about how we and they might work on our differences together.

Legitimacy. No one wants to be treated unfairly. A potentially powerful element in any conflict is an external standard of legitimacy, such as precedent, law, or the principle of reciprocity, which can be used to convince one or more parties that an outcome is fair. This is particularly true wherever constituents are important — and that is so in most cases, whether one's constituents consist of a spouse, a business partner, or the general public. What criteria will a leader on each side be able to use to persuade constituents that an agreed result is legitimate?

One of the strengths of the American judicial system is that it offers two external standards of legitimacy. First, judges look to "the law" — not just to their own subjective feelings but to statutes, precedents, and doctrine — in forming their decisions. Second, the process is designed to be impartial. Parties "have their day in court." Losing parties regularly abide by court judgments, at least in part because the process is seen to be legitimate even when the hearing does not produce the desired outcome.

In coping with an international conflict, it is a good idea to look for external standards of legitimacy, such as pre-existing treaties, customary international law, equality, or most-favored-nation treatment. It is also wise to consider how a fair process, such as impartial fact-finding, neutral recommendations, or arbitration, might produce results that would be acceptable because the process itself would be widely recognized as legitimate.

Alternatives. When negotiating a natural gas agreement with Mexico in 1975, the United States was confident that Mexico would eventually settle for a relatively low price. After all, the United States was the only market readily accessible by pipeline. By focusing on the negative economic consequences to Mexico of not accepting their low offer, the United States negotiators ignored the possibility that Mexican officials would simply refuse to enter into an agreement which they perceived as illegitimate. The Mexican government burned off tens of millions of dollars' worth of natural gas at the wellheads, as a dramatic gesture of independence, before the United States agreed to a price substantially higher than that which it had previously offered.

Consistently, people tend to underestimate the costs to themselves of not reaching agreement and to overestimate the costs to the other side. They fail to think clearly about what they will do if no agreement is reached. We invented the concept of BATNA, the Best Alternative To a Negotiated Agreement, to address this specific problem. Our BATNA is what we walk away to if we cannot reach an agreement with the other side. It is our self-help alternative. But the fact that the other side has a terrible BATNA — for the Mexican government in the example above, it was to waste the gas rather than sell it at an insultingly low price — does not always mean they will agree to our terms.

When estimating our own and the other side's BATNA, ask whether the parties understand the full consequences of failing to resolve the conflict. Are the alternatives to agreement that each party believes it has realistic? Is either being overly optimistic about its domestic support? Military strength? Do the parties appreciate the economic and other costs of carrying on the dispute?

Relationship. It is common to equate good relations with affection, agreement, or a shared outlook. Yet in a conflict situation, we are not concerned with affection or shared values but with an ability to deal well with differences. Maintaining a good working relationship with friends and allies is often easy. Maintaining such a relationship with those with whom we have serious differences, however difficult, is likely to be more important. The more serious our differences, the more crucial it is to be able to deal well with them.

Successive U.S. administrations have found this principle compelling when dealing with the potentially rich markets of the People's Republic of China, and eminently forgettable when dealing with difficult but poor nations like Cuba or Nicaragua. The principle applies with equal force to each, however. Very often the better the working relationship we have with our adversaries, the better able we are to meet our own interests.

Lord Caradon, then the British Ambassador to the United Nations, told us that when he was drafting what became Security Council Resolution 242 of November 1967 on the Middle East (according to which Israel would return occupied territories to Arab rule in exchange for peace, recognition, and security guarantees), the Soviet representative asked him to postpone the Security Council vote for two days. When Caradon replied that although he did not know whether the Soviet Union planned to veto the resolution, abstain, or support it, he was unwilling to give the Soviet Union two more days, the Soviet representative responded that he may have mispoken or been misunderstood. It was not his government that was asking for two days. He, personally, was making the request. Caradon immediately granted it. Although he did not trust the government of the Soviet Union, he had complete confidence that the human being with whom he was dealing would not personally request something that would injure Lord Caradon's interests.

Two days later the Soviet Union voted for Resolution 242, making it unanimous. Caradon's trust in the individual had been well placed. The Soviet representative had used the two days to obtain the instructions that Caradon wished. Whatever the relationship, trusting someone else is always a matter of assessing the risk. That risk may be influenced more by a personal working relationship than an institutional one.

In diagnosing a conflict we will want to look at the state of the relationship. What relationship did the parties have prior to this conflict? Are they likely to have future dealings? What is the level of confidence each party has in the reliability of the other? Each negotiator?

Communication. In Chapter 3, we discussed problems presented by incomplete or ambiguous messages communicated from one party to another. The importance of good communication is illustrated by the case of the USS *Mayaguez,* an American merchant ship captured off the coast of Thailand. In May 1975, twelve days after the fall of the U.S.-supported government of South Vietnam, and twenty-four days after the seizure of power in Cambodia by the communist Khmer Rouge, a Khmer Rouge gunboat seized the *Mayaguez.* The Khmer government claimed that the boat was on a spy mission for the United States and was captured inside Cambodian territorial waters. President Gerald Ford called the seizure "an act of piracy on the high seas" and threatened the most serious consequence unless the ship was released. In response, a Cambodian communiqué argued that a number of CIA spy ships disguised as fishing boats had recently been seized, but indicated that the ship would nonetheless be released shortly.

Neither communiqué mentioned the *Mayaguez* crew. Worried for their safety, President Ford and Secretary of State Henry Kissinger ordered a military rescue mission to proceed. Marines soon landed on Tang Island. They ran into heavy resistance and forty-one of them were killed there and in a related helicopter crash, while many others were wounded. The United States later found and seized the ship, but the crew was not there.

As it turned out, the crew of the *Mayaguez* had been released about an hour before this action began. They said they had been well treated and that they had in fact delayed their own release for twelve hours. They had wanted to avoid sailing at night, partly out of fear that the United States might attack their transport boat or use tear gas against it, as had happened when they were seized. Lives and money were wasted because of poorly designed channels of communication, even though the "rescue mission" and attendant punitive actions were a public relations success in the United States.

Do the parties articulate their perceptions and interests, or do they depend on the other side to guess or know? Do they communicate directly, or are their words filtered through intermediaries and the media? Can the parties communicate in confidence, or must they always play to the grandstand? Are there mechanisms in place to check whether what was understood is in fact what was intended?

Commitment. What commitments would it take to settle a conflict, and what existing commitments may make that difficult? Do parties know when a decision is needed? Can each party articulate exactly what they would like others to agree to? Do they know what others would like them to agree to? If agreement is reached, would compliance require the cooperation of absent parties or the occurrence of events outside the parties' control?

Parties are often asked to commit early and publicly to what they will and will not do. If they do so, each subsequent move in the negotiation is likely to be seen as a strategically difficult and politically costly concession. When U.S. Secretary of State Alexander Haig attempted to mediate the Falklands/Malvinas crisis, he focused public attention on the positions taken by Argentina and Great Britain. Through this process, the two countries' respective demands for "sovereignty" and "withdrawal" became deeper commitments and the possibility of retreat more and more embarrassing. Shuttling across the Atlantic, Secretary Haig then asked if they would commit to some new proposals. Having set out extreme official positions, and feeling reluctant to give up more than was absolutely necessary — at least without knowing what they would receive in return — each side said no. Argentinean officials then expressed surprise when Secretary Haig abruptly abandoned his efforts. They had been expecting later opportunities to make concessions. By emphasizing commitments so early in the process, Haig had made it difficult for the parties to appreciate each other's interests and to explore options that might possibly reconcile those interests.

Parties often fall into the trap of thinking about disputes in terms of a limited number of variables defined by their respective positions. To do so limits their ability to diagnose what is wrong and to move toward fixing it. By using the Seven Elements to analyze why a conflict is not being settled, we can expand our thinking about ways to deal with that conflict.

Use Some Additional Maps

Once we have a sense of the obstacles to progress, we can generate fresh approaches by employing the specialized perspectives of a variety of academic and professional disciplines, using a tool we call the Atlas of Approaches. Collecting many different maps into an atlas reduces the danger that we will be misled by the distortions of any one of them. Academic disciplines and professional points of view can provide us with insights about what is wrong, what is causing it, who could make a difference, and what variables may be manipulable. The list presented in Chart 19 can get us started.

It is sometimes enough simply to imagine, as we do in Chart 20, how a particular discipline or profession might view a conflict. Actual investigation is usually better.

19. An Atlas of Approaches

Maps for Understanding a Conflict

Academic disciplines	Professional points of view
Economics	Religious leader
Political science	Lawyer
Psychology	Doctor
Anthropology	Military officer
History	Journalist
Sociology	Public health official
Business	Diplomat
Ethics	Educator
Engineering	Banker-investor
Geography	Social worker

Adding additional maps or points of view to our atlas helps us better understand a conflict. By identifying the choices available to people who may be able to bring about change, an atlas may help us develop an action plan. Whether we are reading books or speaking with professionals, two kinds of questions are useful to ask: "Why is the conflict not being settled?" And "Who do you think might be able to do what in order to help resolve it?" These questions are sufficiently open-ended to avoid prejudging what we need to learn and at the same time produce ideas of practical use.

Work on the Problem Together

The tools described in this chapter can provide valuable insight to a single individual who is sitting alone, thinking. We often use the tools that way, and suggest that you do, too. Good inventing can be a solitary activity in which we produce fresh ideas by

20. Atlas of Approaches

Case: Fragmentation in Russia, 1993

As a military officer might see it:

What's the problem? (Quadrant I)
  Military leadership at odds with political leadership
  Other republics represent potential threats and drains on resources
  Changes in geopolitical situation diminish need for military
What might be done? (Quadrant III)
  More effective liaison between political factions and military
  Create mutual nonaggression pacts
  Retrain military personnel for internal security measures, such as attacking
    organized crime

As a political analyst might see it:

What's the problem? (Quadrant I)
  Fragmented leadership
  Rising regionalism
  Communist party decline created power vacuum
What might be done? (Quadrant III)
  Integrated, unified leadership
  Establish confederation supporting explicit mutual assistance
  Democratically elected government

As a communication expert might see it:

What's the problem? (Quadrant I)
  Local media coverage of events is ineffective; people don't know what's
    happening
  News is inaccurate and disseminated slowly
  Country lacks widespread modern communication technology
What might be done? (Quadrant III)
  Import some BBC experts
  Reuters or AP expands offices in area, hires locals, trains them
  Full privatization of media
  Joint business ventures between Russian media consortium and Western
    technology groups

asking ourselves different questions. One person, thinking hard, can often produce better ideas than those that come out of a typical meeting. Yet the potential creativity of a group exceeds that of any individual. So why is it that groups often fail to be creative?

To understand why a group is failing to solve a puzzle, it helps to make explicit those constraints that have been implicit, and then to question each one carefully. "Think outside of constraints" is another piece of advice that is easy to say and difficult to implement. Writing out an actual list suggests group norms that could perhaps be relaxed. It may point us toward more promising approaches. Chart 21 suggests how such a comparison might appear for a typical diplomatic conference or meeting.

The substantive product we envision is a wide range of new ideas — some useful, some less so. One single idea that holds the promise of a breakthrough makes the creation of a long list worthwhile. To maximize the chance that a group will produce fresh ideas, it helps to have a session in which that is explicitly understood to be the purpose. It also helps to have some guidelines or norms of behavior that enhance the likelihood of achieving it. We want a brainstorming process that reflects our advice to leave pre-existing constraints behind.

"Brainstorming" is a much-abused term in professional circles these days. Sometimes it is used to mean little more than having an idea. What we mean by brainstorming as a tool for generating fresh ideas is a clearly defined activity with specific ground rules and with theory underlying each step — a theory which helps us break free of some of the constraints we have been discussing.

If proposals are rejected unless they immediately appeal to most participants, each new approach will fail unless it falls within that small area consistent with the current thinking of most members of the group. Instead of garnering the benefits of many

21. Implicit Constraints on Meetings and How to Loosen Them

Rules often followed	Alternative approaches
Wear business attire.	Try a more casual setting.
Do not invite anyone without official status.	Are there others who might contribute?
Rarely meet privately, one on one, with someone from the other delegation.	Could we engineer some time for off-the-record discussions among the principals?
Rotate the chair among involved partisans.	Should we consider a third-party neutral?
Sit across a table facing each other.	Maybe side-by-side would establish a better context.
Keep a verbatim transcript.	No note-taking at all.
Make no remarks except those that reflect official views and for which there is official clearance.	Could we arrange a session where no position was official?
Devote sessions to making arguments, stating positions, and criticizing others.	Could we devote a session only to new ideas?

Often we are constrained from generating new ideas simply by the rules we implicitly impose on our own dialogue. Different norms, such as those in the right-hand column, can create an atmosphere more conducive to brainstorming.

minds and many perspectives, we tend to limit one another. Effort is wasted, and we hear muttering about "too many cooks."

We want to establish a context where we can reap the benefits of everyone's creative thinking and take advantage of diverse perspectives, without risking the cumulative impact of negative or skeptical views. Folklorists see many cooks as an advantage; they say that it takes four people to make a salad: a spendthrift to pour the oil, a miser to pour the vinegar, a wise elder to season it, and a lunatic to toss it.

The process of problem-solving similarly benefits when a team of participants can each bring their particular talents. We may want to create special roles, like facilitator, recorder, and time-keeper. Most conducive to generating new ideas is an environment in which wild ideas are encouraged, even ideas that are in fact well outside the realm of the possible. When chosen for the post of Secretary General of the United Nations, Boutros Boutros-Ghali observed, "If I lost hope every time I proposed something offbeat, I would never have accomplished anything."

Suppose we have three members in our group, who are reasonable people with assumptions as to what is realistic, as indicated by the three overlapping ellipses in Chart 22. If the members of the group focus only on ideas that everyone will accept, they will come up with only the lowest common denominator, as indicated by the shaded area. What is actually possible and workable can be indicated by some such area as that contained within the circle in the chart.

To design an occasion that encourages creative thinking within this larger area requires new rules. One good rule is "no negative criticism" during the brainstorming stage. Even casual criticism may inhibit wild idea "W" in Chart 22 and in turn have a chilling effect on the entire creative process. Later, when there is a long list of ideas, there will be an appropriate time to evaluate and improve upon or abandon them. Experience with brainstorming sessions leads us to recommend the guidelines listed in Chart 23.

The facilitator of a brainstorming session is charged with engendering as many new ideas as possible, while still focusing efforts on the problem at hand. Having participants sit side by side in an informal semicircle, facing a white board or series of flip charts, often helps them attack the problem rather than one another.

22. Generate Fresh Ideas through Brainstorming

The Case for Being Open to Wild Ideas

A, B, and C are three participants. The solid ellipses represent their respective working assumptions as to the outer limits of what they each believe might be possible. Only those ideas falling within the shaded area would be initially acceptable to all three participants. What is actually possible would be all ideas falling within some such area as that indicated by the circle.

If the participants open themselves to wild ideas, wild idea W might in turn spark new idea N from someone else. This new idea, which would also prove to be unworkable, might stimulate a creative combination of W and N, hybrid idea H, which is outside what each thought feasible, but still inside the real limit of possibilities.

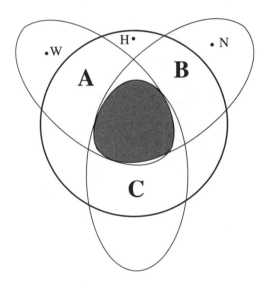

Idea H would never have been conceived had the members of the group considered only those ideas that everyone would initially accept.

23. Some Guidelines for Brainstorming

Schedule a special occasion, assemble a few people (between five and ten is ideal), and identify the time as a session to be devoted solely to coming up with new ideas.

Make it clear that it is to be a meeting at which no proposals are to be agreed upon nor decisions made.

The circumstances of the session should be substantially different from those of routine meetings. It may be held, for example, at an unusual time (evening, all day, a weekend), at an unusual place (country house, outdoors, social club), or under unusual conditions (no scheduled breaks for coffee or meals, participants stand or sit on the floor).

Consider breaking a large group down into smaller working groups tackling different aspects of the problem simultaneously.

The rules of discussion should preclude negative comments. This should be strictly enforced, especially in the early part of a session.

It should be clear that value is placed on developing many new and different ideas. Consider devising incentives to reward abundant creative thinking.

Ideas are recorded on one central list, such as a white board or flip chart, where they are visible to all (so that they may stimulate other ideas), but they are "off the record" and listed without attribution — no list is kept of who came up with what idea.

Use a facilitator and someone to record every idea on the board or flip chart. (These roles can be filled by one person, but it is easier with two.) They can step out of role temporarily to contribute their own ideas to the list.

Schedule a separate session for evaluating and criticizing ideas and selecting the most promising ones for follow-up discussions.

There are particular rewards in having participants from opposite sides face a conflict as a common problem. The joint generation of fresh and unexpected ideas can constitute a significant step in changing the game from oppositional conflict to one of cooperation in the task of coping with it. But sometimes those whom we would like to invite to a brainstorming session, including some people from "the other side" of a conflict, might face formidable constraints on their participation. It is useful to include participants representing varied points of view or having a specialized understanding of different facets of a conflict. Those individuals most able to enlighten us may, however, have difficulty receiving authority to attend, or may themselves worry about how their ideas would be interpreted or exploited by others. Skillful framing of an invitation, along with sensitivity to such limitations, can help overcome these barriers.

Chart 24 is one formulation of a draft invitation to a type of brainstorming session we call a Devising Session. Such a draft invitation can be presented to potential invitees for their comments or criticism *before* an invitation is actually extended. This sort of an "off-the-record" Devising Session, possibly held after an informal meal in a private home, is intended to encourage parties jointly to invent new ideas at low risk.

There are a variety of less structured ways of getting parties together for some creative thinking. To overcome resistance, a proposed gathering can be identified as "exploratory," "pre-negotiation," "off-the-record," "without commitment," or "without prejudice." It can also be stated that no commitment of any kind will be sought or given. An invitation that proposes a specific time and place makes it easier to accept. To make it sound less unilateral, one can add "or would you suggest some other time and place that may be more convenient for you?"

Whatever the occasion is called, the goal is to generate a wide range of ideas before we narrow them down. At the Harvard Negotiation Project and Conflict Management Group, we sponsored a series of Devising Sessions on El Salvador during the civil war there. Several Salvadoran midcareer officials and business professionals attended these sessions while they were in Cambridge to work on Harvard degrees, along with a former

24. Draft Invitation to a Devising Session

The following document is a draft on which we would like your advice without commitment of any kind. It is not yet a proposal. We contemplate that it will go through several revisions in light of comments, criticism, and suggestions. If there appears to be sufficient interest in the general idea, we may well issue an invitation.

1. It is widely recognized that something should be done about the _____ problem.

2. You are invited to participate in an informal working session to generate proposals that one or more participants might wish to recommend to others.

3. Participation in the session and whatever is said there are wholly without prejudice to the positions of any party.

4. It is not contemplated that any decisions will be taken at the working session.

5. Participants will seek, side by side, to generate a useful list of:

   (a) symptoms and problems that may need attention;

   (b) possible causes of these problems;

   (c) general approaches and prescriptive ideas that may merit consideration;

   (d) proposals for specific action that one or more participants might wish to recommend that someone undertake in the near future.

6. Each person who receives this invitation may invite one additional person whose insight might prove valuable. To avoid the session's becoming too large for constructive brainstorming, it is suggested that invitees consult with us before enlarging the group.

7. The proposed list of invitees is:

   [please suggest names]

We propose circulating a draft invitation, and collaborating with potential invitees about the guest list. This kind of informal, consultative process can help prospective participants overcome some internal political constraints they may be facing to attending a session where members of "the other side" will be present.

State Department official, an American journalist, a midlevel official from the Mexican government, and several process consultants with experience in other Central American conflicts. The sessions were initiated and facilitated by a law student. The ideas generated led to several working visits to El Salvador and Costa Rica. Parties on both sides considered the work helpful in getting the U.N.-mediated peace process off the ground.

Generate Some Action Ideas

The tools we present in this volume are of limited value if they are employed merely to diagnose obstacles to resolving an entrenched conflict. Each of the analytical tools can also be used, either on our own or in a group, to stimulate suggestions as to who might do what next. When there are misperceptions, what might be done to correct them? Where high emotions are impeding rational progress, how might they be dealt with? What interests behind our respective positions look potentially reconcilable, and which differences might be exploited? Where people appear to be receiving an ineffective message, how might what is being said be better formulated or better communicated? What are the rules of the game we are currently playing, and how could they be changed?

Just as a carpenter will not always use a hammer, a saw, and a screwdriver in a particular order, there is no one right way to organize and use these tools. At the Harvard Negotiation Project we use a number of different methods of putting these tools into practice. One way to coordinate the results of a variety of analytical approaches is to prepare a checklist of tools and to note opposite each a diagnostic insight that was gained, or a prescriptive approach that it suggested, or both. A second way to pull things together is to use the Four-Quadrant Analysis, looking at each quadrant in turn and restating our present thinking on (I) the symptoms with which we are dealing, (II) the basic diagnosis of what is lacking or is causing those symptoms, (III) the general approach that theory suggests, and (IV) the specific action program that applies that theory to the real world. A third way to proceed is to use the Seven Elements as our primary template for organizing our thoughts, and to brainstorm using the Four-Quadrant tool under the heading of each element.

Placing such diagnostic analyses before a group provides stimulating grist for inventing. It may also prompt us to refocus our efforts. An analysis of partisan perceptions in the communal conflict in Northern Ireland, for example, might suggest that our efforts are better spent shaping attitudes of young people through changes in education than trying to end the conflict by controlling the combatants. An analysis of the currently perceived choice of the Turkish Cypriot Rauf Denktash of Northern Cyprus suggests that there is little that we can offer him likely to be more attractive than what he now has: the presidency, albeit of an unrecognized territory. (A settlement with the Greek Cypriots would probably yield him, at best, the vice presidency or a very short term as president.) If this is the case, we need to explore unilateral measures, or the option of influencing a different party, such as the Greek or Turkish government, to play a more active role. A broad view of what may be wrong in a conflict should produce an equally broad view of the strategies we might pursue.

At each stage in the process, proposed options should be considered tentative. Any one approach needs to be used concurrently with others. Insights gained and decisions made should cause us to revisit previous thinking. An action plan is not something that can be generated in a linear fashion, one step at a time. It often involves putting together elements as disparate as those of a Hollywood film: actors, script, producer, director, financing, camera crew, and so forth. Making decisions along the way calls for intuition, common sense, experience, and judgment. In moving from broad approach to detailed application, we are going to have to proceed by cutting and fitting, by trial and error, and by considering changes to our ideas until what we propose makes sense.

Fresh ideas are the most useful when crossing from the realm of diagnosis into the realm of prescription. Hard work is required to carry the most constructive and promising ideas all the way through Quadrant IV of a Four-Quadrant Analysis — that is, down to the level of specificity where it is clear who does what tomorrow morning. For an action plan to emerge that is worth pursuing, all diagnoses and potential prescriptive advice should fit together in a plausible way. The key task is to figure out what our side should do in order to change the choice faced by others, and to present for their consideration a proposal that would do so, meeting both their interests and ours.

Choosing to help cope with a conflict doesn't have to be heroic. It can mean acting as a facilitator when a group is stuck or sending around a memo asking for an informal meeting of your department to check and revise some crippling working assumptions. It can mean being proactive at meetings and offering to record what the group is saying on a flip chart or white board, or even just cleaning up the coffee cups when the meeting is over. It means not assuming that things will just happen without you.

5

Formulate
Good Advice

Time and again, those involved in an international conflict — or in any conflict — fail to convert their goal into a decision they would like an adversary to make. Although we often think of ourselves as attempting to influence an adversary, we rarely think out just what kind of a decision our side might reasonably expect of the other. For years, those who organized political violence on behalf of the Palestinian cause failed to formulate a plausible decision that an Israeli government might make in response to that violence. From the Israeli point of view, such violence killed fewer Israelis than were being killed by reckless drivers on the highway from Jerusalem to Tel Aviv. It was terrible, but there was no realistic decision that could bring it to an end. Palestinians offered Israelis a problem, not a solution.

After sketching out how the choice appears to the other side and then creating an action plan to improve the situation, we need to focus next on how our action plan might become reality. So often we have a bright idea that never goes anywhere because it is not a plan *for* someone, even when it maps out a constructive process. We fail to translate our plan into an action that someone could take tomorrow. It is time to turn a general idea into a question to be presented to the other side. What are some specific decisions that we might want and might reasonably expect a decisionmaker on the other side to make? Instead of simply confronting them with a problem, we should identify one or more specific actions that we would like them to take to deal with that problem.

Is Our Proposal "Yesable"?

We can increase the likelihood that our idea will be translated into constructive action by estimating the path our proposal will have to travel on its way to implementation, and who along the way will need to be persuaded. We can run our proposal through several checklists to test it for different kinds of feasibility, both practical and ethical. Even if we are acting as advisers to ourselves, it is usually worth checking our ideas. We may be able to anticipate a potential roadblock and figure out how to overcome it.

To check our work, we ask whether we have constructed a choice to which the answer yes meets three tests:

- Yes is a sufficient answer;
- Yes is a realistic answer; and
- Yes is operational.

While these criteria may seem at first glance to be expressing the same idea, in fact they are quite different.

Yes is sufficient. We need to offer others a way forward instead of yet another problem. They should see themselves as having a specific option before them — something to which a simple affirmative is an adequate response. President Lyndon Johnson wanted memos that crossed his desk to end up with a proposal and with a choice of boxes at the bottom for him to check: "Yes," "No," or "See me." He did not want staff to bring him a problem without taking the additional step of suggesting something that could be done about it.

Yes is realistic. Formulating a yesable proposition is no guarantee that the other party will in fact say yes. There should be a good chance that the proposition will be acceptable. Perhaps the chance is not as high as "more likely than not" — but yes should be at least a significant possibility. We are not looking for a guarantee of success but rather for something worth trying for. Depending on how high the stakes are and the effort required on our part, an estimated one-in-five chance of success may well be enough. The more that a proposal meets a party's interests, the more likely it is to be accepted. In order to judge the likelihood of the other side's agreeing to our proposal, we can look back at the Target Future Choice chart discussed in Chapter 3. At that time, we outlined the consequences that a proposal — the X Plan — should produce in order for the other side to say yes. We want to confirm that there is a fair likelihood the other side would agree to it.

Yes is operational. If our target decisionmaker agrees with our proposal, *something happens.* Some specific action, such as a ceasefire, a meeting, or the appointment of a representative, will take place. Rarely does it make sense to ask for a mere statement of principle: "Yes, we agree that peace is important." It is better to have any such statement or principle accompanied by an operational decision that tells us who will do what when: ". . . and we hereby agree to attend the meeting proposed for next week."

The more clearly we know the parameters of the specific decision that we want and might expect, the more likely we are to obtain it. In order to understand those parameters, it is helpful to write out drafts of the very words that we might like another party to accept. We can try writing out several alternative versions in varying degrees of detail. A particularly valuable challenge is to draft a brief statement which their decisionmaker might sign, or make public, or send as instructions to some subordinate official. Such a draft, written in the first person using the decisionmaker's voice, also reinforces the practice of putting ourselves in the other person's shoes.

Whom Should We Attempt to Persuade?

Our proposed decisionmaker is our "target of influence," meaning that we are trying to persuade that person to do something differently. Are we seeking to have the President of South Africa do something about the situation there, or would the executive director of a citizen's action committee be a better choice? The person we choose is a "point of choice" — the Prince we would be writing to if we were Machiavelli. The "something" they will do differently amounts to the substance of our proposal. A sound approach to choosing whom we want to influence is first to generate a range of possible targets and then to select from among them. Generating such a list frees us from any fixed view about who it is that we should be trying to influence. A checklist of categories of people and organizations to consider may be helpful.

Let's say that we are would-be peacemakers dealing with the violence in the former Yugoslavia, specifically the ethnic strife in Bosnia, where Muslims, Croats, and Serbs have been wrangling over boundary lines that will separate their respective communities. Looking for points of choice where decisions might be made that could reduce the violence, we consider a broad range of potential targets of influence. They might be on one side of the conflict or another, or they might be third parties. For the situation in Bosnia we might, for example, assume that we are advising the head of an American group that wants to phase out the communal violence. Say that we have devised a plan whereby a small, private, intercommunal school would be opened in Sarajevo, designed to accommodate the dozens and dozens of children of "mixed" Bosnian marriages: Muslim-Serb, Serb-Croat, and Muslim-Croat. (As the daughter of a Croat and a Serb explained it, proposals physically to separate the three communities assume that Bosnians of mixed ancestry "are nothing at all." She dreams of what she calls a neutral republic. Now she is worried about how and where she can raise her children.)

If we have no fixed advisee, we may be looking for one. In these circumstances, any person on our list of significant decisionmakers is a potential target of influence. An important feature of such a list is that each entry on it should be a unit — someone or some entity that in fact makes decisions. "All American companies investing in Eastern and Central Europe" would not be a point of choice since no choice is made by that group acting jointly; companies investing in an entire region do not sit down together and reach a decision.

Prescriptive advice often assumes that large groups could solve a problem if only "they" would decide to behave in a certain way. "If Americans would stop being so ethnocentric, the world would be a better place." "If international news media devoted less attention to political violence, there would be less incentive to commit it." But Americans do not jointly decide how ethnocentric to be. Nor do the international news media reach a collective decision on how much time and space to devote to the reporting of political violence. Such advice fails to focus on a point of choice.

From among the names on our list we tentatively select the most promising candidate — the one our future efforts will be intended to persuade. In the light of further work we may change our minds and decide to work on somebody else, but as we go about the task of designing a target choice it is helpful to have in mind at all times, at least provisionally, some specific point where that choice could be made. The exercise of selecting a decision-maker can itself serve to clarify a complicated problem by organizing it in terms of the possible actions of specific players.

If we are seeking to influence a group, such as a committee, a cabinet, or a board of directors which formally acts as a decisional unit, it may still help to think in terms of directing our efforts toward one person within that group — ideally somebody who could take the initiative and then be able to carry the rest of the group along. We will want to think of what that person will need in order to be persuaded, and then of the arguments that he or she will need in order to convince others. Issues of group dynamics and organizational behavior will affect any single decisionmaker selected, and there are, of course, limits to how much one can account for such factors. We are not trying to predict what that person will in fact do. Rather, we have picked this person as someone who could probably make a difference if they could be persuaded to do so.

If this process of selecting a point of choice has resulted in our focusing on a person other than the one that we were treating as our presumptive adversary, we should now construct a Currently Perceived Choice chart for this new person. For example, if we have decided to give up on the Bosnian President and to work on someone else instead, then we should prepare a list of estimated consequences which we use to illuminate the currently perceived choice of the person we have selected.

How Do We Reach the Decisionmaker?

So far in this book we have been looking at international conflict through the eyes of a player. Implicit in this perspective is the assumption that we are able to deliver our advice directly and on our own. Most likely, however, we will not be in that position for one of several reasons: either (1) we are not part of the diplomatic and political hierarchy; (2) even if we have an official position, we may not be able to put our action plan in front of the other side; or (3) for strategic reasons, we may not want to be the one to present our proposal to the other side. (These three categories probably encompass almost everybody, with the possible exceptions of the U.N. Secretary-General and the Pope.)

We believe that even a private citizen lacking the obvious platform of a political office or academic appointment can become an activist promoting a clear and cogent action plan through a series of carefully chosen intermediaries (even if that advice, like the advice we at the Harvard Negotiation Project give, is often rejected). The key is discovering someone who can serve as our "entry point" into the decisionmaking process. Usually this first intermediary will be someone we know or someone with whom we have had contact. If we know Nelson Mandela, great, we'll just hand him our proposal the next time we see him. But most of the time, most of us must take a more indirect route. For students, a pathway to a decisionmaker may be through a professor. Other routes include a state or federal congressional representative, a local political or lobbying organization, or a business or media contact.

Often, the entry point will not know our target decisionmaker directly but will need to go through a series of decisionmakers. Therefore, an important first step is to convince the entry point of the wisdom of our action program so that he will forward it on to a decisionmaker. In other words, we have at least three layers of people we need to persuade: the entry point, so he will pass our work along, the intermediate decisionmaker, and the final decisionmaker whose behavior is the ultimate target of our efforts. But often there will be a fourth or fifth person through whom the proposal must pass, and who must be persuaded of its viability.

Obviously, before contacting our first decisionmaker, we need to consider what she will have to do to follow our advice. Let's say our chosen decisionmaker is Senator Kassebaum in the case of former Yugoslavia, as illustrated in Chart 25. The presentation of our new action plan to the other side will clearly put her on the line as well. Therefore, we need to think through how the plan will appear to her and, perhaps most importantly, how she will appear to others. Why would it be in her interest to try to get the other side to see the problem in a new way?

To help answer this question, we can construct a simple balance sheet asking, from the point of view of our decisionmaker, "Should I accept the recommended action plan and forward it along?" We have given her a yesable proposition from the point of view of the ultimate decisionmaker, but is it one to which, from her point of view, she ought to say yes? What might be the negative aspects of implementing the action plan? Presumably there are costs in terms of time and effort. There may also be some predictable negative reactions from others, or costs in terms of precedent or reputation. A rigorous look at the balance sheet of our entry point is advisable before we convert our bright idea into a recommendation.

25. Putting an Idea into Action

I

Analyze a conflict, formulate advice, and transmit that advice in the form of a suggested action program to a decisionmaker on our side, often by means of an "entry point," someone with access to the decisionmaker.
[Say I take my ideas on the conflict in the former Yugoslavia and write them up into a short, persuasive memo.]

Entry point

1

The entry point is convinced of the merit of my action program, and he forwards the advice on to our decisionmaker.
[I mail my memo, along with a cover letter, to an aide of Senator Kassebaum and follow up with a phone call.]

2

Our decisionmaker

The decisionmaker receives the advice and, if she agrees with the recommendation, decides to implement the action program. The implementation of the action program results in presenting a new choice, however small, to a decisionmaker on the other side.
[Senator Kassebaum reads my memo along with her aide's recommendation that the action plan be implemented. She now has a new suggestion to present, for example, to a Yugoslavian educator in a position to take action.]

3

Their decisionmaker

The decisionmaker on the other side considers this new proposal which, combined with other developments independent of us, changes the choice he sees himself facing so that he can now say yes to this proposal although he has resisted others.
[The action program, much modified by the hands it has been through, is now transmitted to local school boards in a position to do something about implementing it.]

26. Target Future Choice of a Decisionmaker

"Shall I now propose the X Plan to the other side?"

Consequences if I say YES

+ The X plan meets my interests.

+ I need not abandon any prior position.

+ If the X plan succeeds, I get credit and my influence grows.

+ If the X plan fails, I can avoid blame.

+ I keep my options open, and can propose, or not propose, other solutions in the future.

+ It is easy. All I have to do is sign a letter.

+ There is a chance of success.

+ One issue is (at least partially) resolved.

Consequences if I say NO

− I have little chance for recognition.

− I miss a fading opportunity.

− There will be more obstacles in the future.

BUT

+ I have not abandoned my position.

Earlier, we looked at the Target Future Choice chart for a decisionmaker on the other side — what elements would be necessary to construct a yesable proposition for *them?* We now want to use the same tool for our own intermediary. Filled out with our action plan from the former Yugoslavia example, we ask: Should Senator Kassebaum agree to propose our advice to a decisionmaker on the other side? Chart 26 is a general example of our decisionmaker's target future choice.

Components of a New Choice

Let's say that a decisionmaker on our side has received our proposal from the entry point and has decided to implement the suggested action plan. This plan will often take the form of presenting a new choice, however small, to someone on the other side. One way for us to measure the viability of our proposal is to assess whether it has *changed the choice* the other side sees itself as facing. Ideally, the new choice is one to which the other side can now say yes, even though it had been resisting other options in the past.

But the other side is full of multiple layers of decisionmakers, too. And many people feel a natural reluctance to making a decision that can easily be put off. It is useful to remind ourselves of this by framing the decision we are asking for as an immediate one: "Shall I today agree that . . ." or, "Shall I now . . ." Sometimes the decision we have been trying to get someone else to make could be postponed without cost. Decisions are far more likely to be accepted if they offer a fading opportunity.

A viable action plan does not have to be specific on every point. We may conclude that there should be silence or ambiguity surrounding some elements of our proposed decision. But that should be the result of a conscious strategy, not muddy thinking. We should have explicit reasons for being silent; clear and cogent reasons for being ambiguous. For example, leaving the long-term resolution of the West Bank ambiguous in an invitation for talks made Israel and the Palestinians more willing to talk. Explicitly addressing one of the most contentious issues before the parties are even at the table, along the lines of, "We invite you to a meeting to decide on the sovereign independence of the West Bank," would have ensured that one crucial party to the dispute would not show up.

How an idea is to be transmitted to the proposed decisionmaker is an important question. If we are involved in a dispute with another nation, direct communication from our side may look like an ultimatum in which they have had no input. Perhaps the suggestion should come from a third party. Even so, we should see what we can come up with working on our own. At a minimum, we have some information about decisions that would satisfy us. We can decide later whether it is prudent to transmit them ourselves or wiser to try to work through a third party.

The Morality of Persuasion

Before contacting an entry point or passing an action plan along to a decisionmaker, we should pause to make sure that the advice we have generated — even though it has a chance of being accepted — is advice we really want to give. Cold calculations about the rational conduct of international affairs seem to drain the humanity out of the way we relate to one other. Rather than helping to promote a cooperative world community based on human fellowship, logical deductions can lead to amoral, if not immoral, actions that often look like the mechanical manipulation of others. Is there no more to carrying out foreign policy than pure pragmatism? There are evil and selfish people in the world; are we supposed to become intimate and friendly colleagues of theirs? Should we do business with those who persistently and seriously violate human rights? How do we compare the merits of "taking a stand" with the merits of trying to bring about some marginal improvement, perhaps in the economic conditions of people who will nonetheless remain at the mercy of merciless leaders?

In international relations, each government faces difficult choices when dealing with other governments that may be dictatorial, militant, or repressive. What advice should we give, for example, to a European democracy or to a new African state about how to deal with governments like those of Franco's Spain, Stalin's Soviet Union, Botha's South Africa, or, in recent years, Albania, North Korea, Cambodia, Cuba, Burma, Libya, Haiti, Panama, and so forth? It is said that he who sups with the devil should have a long spoon. Just how is that accomplished in international affairs?

While we focus our efforts on pragmatic questions, we should also try to think with equal rigor about ethical questions. Too often the latter are avoided entirely. Yet to propose in a few pages how moral considerations can be integrated into the conduct of international relations is, in one sense, the height of arrogance or folly. It is to march briskly off where even those who are divinely inspired tread far more circumspectly. On the other hand, to fail to suggest practical ways for bringing ideas about ethics to bear on governmental decisionmaking is to make the powerful statement that ethical considerations are irrelevant. To ignore moral difficulties is to send the wrong message, even if we accept that it is a complex and controversial subject.

Rather than laying out all the ethical pros and cons of different choices, we suggest a process goal: to generate a series of questions such that we will usually be better off in the long run if we ask ourselves those questions, and try to answer them honestly, than if we do not.

For example, one question we might ask to measure the "rightness" of our proposal would be whether it minimizes the chance that we will later regret what we have done. If we make a decision today and later learn from others things that cause us to regret that decision, we have, in one sense, made a mistake. If we had known more, we would not have acted as we did. We can think of our lives as stumbling forward toward increasing knowledge and enlightenment. A reasonable goal, then, is to try to act in such a way that as we learn more we are increasingly likely to believe that we acted properly. By testing our assumptions against the criteria described below, we can try to minimize regrets and maximize the chance that we will continue to believe we did the right thing.

Rational thought should not exclude gut feelings about the "rightness" of a given behavior, but feelings, such as regret, are no substitute for careful consideration of what standards or principles make our proposed plan the right thing to do, what may be wrong with it, and how we propose to resolve such questions.

Morality measured by the conduct itself. Sometimes we may justify or condemn conduct without regard to its consequences. In such circumstances we argue that our conduct is simply the right thing to do, whether or not it ever "does any good." Some things, we insist, are unambiguously wrong (such as turning on the gas in the Nazi gas chambers), even if we became convinced that by doing it ourselves we could do it more humanely or inflict less harm than if we refused and others were to act in our stead. Other conduct, according to this approach, is simply *right* because of the nature of the acts themselves, like voting and refraining from littering, irrespective of a cost-benefit analysis or whether others follow suit.

In such circumstances we judge conduct to be right or wrong independently of a precise calculation of whether the net costs or benefits are expected to outweigh those of pursuing an alternative course of conduct. Feeding a starving man is still good even if letting him starve to death might somehow generate a needed public program that would save more lives in the long run. The act of a pacifist or vegetarian is not to be assessed by its ultimate consequences but rather by the value of the act itself. The actor is asserting that he himself is doing good or avoiding harm, and that is what counts.

Can objective criteria be applied to actions so justified? We should not demand perfect logical consistency. If one who is opposed to killing other life becomes a vegetarian, we score no moral victory by pointing out that he sets mousetraps, wears leather shoes, or swats mosquitoes. Two related tests do seem appropriate. One is the golden rule, that he is treating others as he would like to be treated. The second is that the actor is behaving the way that he would like us all to behave, combined with the belief that if all behaved similarly, that would be good. There is no contention that others will in fact follow the example, but that the act itself is inherently good.

For a long time people have thought that it is moral to behave as one would like others to behave. There may, however, be limits to this approach. Even where an act is justified by itself and not by its consequences, there is probably a moral obligation on the actor to think about possibly harmful consequences and to make sure that they do not outweigh the virtue of the act itself. The rightness of giving alms to a poor beggar may have to be questioned if one is simply supporting an addiction to alcohol or drugs. The virtue of simply giving aid to an impoverished Third World country may be seriously undercut if the consequence of the generosity is to line the pockets of a military warlord.

Morality measured by the consequences. In a conflict situation, the morality of action is frequently measured not by assessing the inherent nature of the act but by weighing its consequences. For example, the morality of a military operation may be measured by the predictable results: What costs fall on whom for what benefit? Beyond criteria for judging when an act is thought to be inherently good or bad, we therefore need criteria for deciding when the end justifies the means.

If, for example, one refuses to talk with communists or terrorists "as a matter of moral principle," one must look for justification of that position not in the act itself but rather in the expected consequences. The argument runs that talking with terrorists rewards bad behavior and may encourage more terrorism. Unlike the arguments discussed in the previous section, it is an argument that has to be based on weighing the probable consequences, since it cannot successfully be argued that the very act of talking is causing direct harm. If everybody stopped talking with terrorists, the harm would not automatically end, as it would if everyone refused to turn on the gas in gas chambers, or refused to fight in a war. In fact, if we had stopped talking to the Soviets, the Cuban missile crisis could well have resulted in a nuclear exchange.

The desirability of clear thinking on ethical questions is illustrated by the debate in recent years over investment in South Africa. It was difficult to argue that receiving a dividend check from a company that invested in South Africa was inherently unethical. It was presumably no more inherently unethical to receive such funds than it was for a black miner in South Africa to receive his wages. But it may well be that by refusing to work in the mine, or by refusing to invest in companies doing business in South Africa, we could produce good results. When the morality of an action depends upon a predicted chain of events, however, one is no longer free to ignore that chain of events. If "washing one's hands" of a problem is defended on the ground that doing so will cause good things to happen, then one needs to look closely at what will in fact happen.

One could argue, for example, that divestment from South Africa was a good idea because of its symbolic value, but only so long as one then went on to test the assumption about the impact of symbolism — and that particular symbolic act — in international politics. One could also argue that divestment from South Africa was wise because hurting the economy could be expected over time to cause its leaders to end apartheid, and that

that potential goal outweighed the economic and social pain being inflicted in the meantime on most of South Africa's poor. This, again, is a quite different argument from asserting that divestment from South Africa was good because white South African leaders were bad people.

In short, if one makes moral decisions based on the possible consequences, there is a moral requirement to be pragmatic — to calculate the probable results of one's action and to assess the good and the bad. Most of this book is devoted to this exercise. Before finishing an action plan and proposing it, we should review the coherence of our theory about what we are doing, run through our ends and our means, and check them against a variety of ethical criteria, as we discuss further below.

Morality measured by society's best windows. The fact that people differ as to what they believe is right and wrong causes some to conclude that there are no standards to which to adhere. Put another way, they conclude that since people differ, preferences among ethical standards are like preferences in food or fashion. Everyone chooses what they like. There is no moral standard out there. But the absence of a single legal standard does not mean that there is no law. That lawyers and judges differ in their interpretations of law in no way suggests that we should not comply with the law. Nor do such differences free judges or lawyers from searching for the best view of the law that they can find, adhering to the law which they believe to be correct, and calling on others to do so.

Ethical standards as such are not governmentally designed or enforced, nor are they interpreted by judges. But ethical standards, like legal ones, cannot be dismissed as irrelevant because of differences of opinion. In fact, it is those very differences which illuminate moral questions and help us address them. A bare statutory rule is nowhere near as illuminating as the combined opinions of a dozen judges dealing with different cases in which a problem covered by the rule has been raised and discussed.

To cope with moral choice, we will want to benefit from the best that our civilization and culture, or that of other cultures with which we can make ourselves familiar, has to offer. Thus one option is to turn for guidance to the humanities, which serve as the repositories of much of the wisdom and experience of human society. To minimize the chance that we will later regret our decision because we have learned more, we will want to make as much use as possible of knowledge that has heretofore been accumulated. The disciplines of history, philosophy, law, religion, political science, and literature each has a lot to say about good and bad standards. No one of them can provide a definitive answer, but each can offer questions that shed light.

A list of possible questions appears in Chart 27. Such questions do not impose an external judgment upon the purpose or action we contemplate as much as they help us think about what we already know. They do not impose somebody else's moral judgment; they help us turn into a moral judgment values which we have already embraced. The process does not guarantee that two individuals, whom we would agree are "equally ethical," will come up with the same conclusions. They may assign different probabilities to what is going to happen, place relatively different emphasis on short-term concerns as contrasted with long-term ones, or value social, economic, or environmental consequences differently.

To judge the morality of one's own, or someone's conduct, we need to have a good idea of the purpose of that action and the process by which the conduct was decided upon. If we know that purposes were carefully selected, that the means were carefully designed to serve those purposes, and that both ends and means were consciously assessed in the light of high standards, that is about as much as we can ask.

27. Some Ethical Criteria to Consider Before Making a Proposal

History

How are future historians likely to judge conduct like this?
If, years hence, I myself look back at this conduct am I more likely to be proud of it or ashamed of it?
Will it be cited to my credit or will I have to defend it?

Philosophy

What are guiding principles of which my proposed action is an application?
Are those principles that I would commend to all?

Law

Is the proposed conduct legal?
Would comparable conduct within most countries be legal?
Would the conduct be consistent with wise laws as they should be established and interpreted?

Religion

Is the proposed conduct consistent with the teachings of the world's religions?
Would the conduct be seen as an example of how a deeply religious person ought to behave?

Political science

Is this policy a wise guide for future actions?
Is the principle behind the policy one we would recommend to others to follow?
Does this policy build on the best policies and principles of the past?

Literature

How would I have to behave so that if a novelist or dramatist were basing a work on this incident I might be the hero of that work?
Is the proposed conduct more like that of literary heroes or literary villains?

Family and friends

Would I be pleased to learn that my mother or father had behaved as I propose to behave?
Would I be proud to learn that my child had behaved this way?
Would I want my children to use this bit of conduct as a guide for their future actions?
If, through no doing of mine, a full account of my proposed conduct appeared on the front page of tomorrow's newspaper, is it more likely that I would be proud or embarrassed?

How Likely Is Our Decisionmaker to Agree to Our Proposal?

Once we conclude that our idea is a good one — however we might measure "goodness" — we can explore its feasibility. It is a difficult task to assess the political viability of a new idea. The real world imposes serious constraints upon the decisions that political leaders and others are in fact willing to make. Faced with the probability that small proposals of a routine nature are more likely to be approved than fresh and unusual suggestions (and working in an environment where ideas are often valued by appearing to be "sound"), bureaucrats tend to overemphasize the restraints on a leader's choice. We can rest assured that it was no bureaucratic underling who suggested that Egyptian President Anwar Sadat fly to Israel or that President Carter commit himself to two solid weeks of a Camp David meeting. Staff tend to assume that political constraints are greater than they are.

So how do we estimate the serious constraints on choice that do exist? In countries with a parliamentary democracy, one might in theory try to count votes. Or one might look to public opinion polls, where they exist. But in all countries, leaders are not wholly confined by public opinion; they have some power to lead.

Any leader who makes a new decision will want to be able to justify it to constituents (whether colleagues or the public) and will be concerned with the criticisms others may advance. One way to get a feel for the plausibility of a proposed decision is to extend the exercise we used for our proposal when we were trying to test whether it would be yesable to the other side. We attempted to draft the very words we would envision the decision-maker accepting. Now we can do the same thing for the decision-maker on our side, to help her deal with her own constituents.

A first step is to write out two or three strong points which she might make in support of her decision. Then write out two or three strong attacks on the decision that might be publicly made by critics. Looking at the extent to which a proposed decision is vulnerable to criticism may help us reformulate it to make it less so. Writing out the strongest statement that we think could be made in support of a decision may also suggest possible improvements. The two sets of statements should help us assess the possibility of persuading the decisionmaker to go ahead.

One persuasive way to present the affirmative case for a decision is to draft the text of a possible public statement announcing it. A few sentences or a couple of paragraphs will often be enough to suggest either that an idea is wholly unrealistic or that it might fly. Before suggesting that Iran and the United States accept Algerian mediation of the 1980 hostage crisis, for example, each government was shown drafts illustrating how each could explain a potential mediated outcome to its constituents (Charts 28 and 29).

To assess the vulnerability of the idea to criticism, we can identify two or three likely critics who can be counted on to publicize their displeasure. If we were drafting a press release for one of them, and wanted to generate a quotable statement for tomorrow's press, what is the worst thing about the decision that they could honestly say? What might other critics say?

Chart 30, using the example of the North American Free Trade Agreement, suggests one way of assessing the political constraints that may keep our decisionmaker from deciding as we would like. Drafting a public announcement of a decision is more than a way to assess existing constraints on choice. It is also a good way to help sell an idea. A decisionmaker is likely to be reluctant to buy an idea unless he sees how it could be persuasively presented to others. In writing such a statement, we will want to look for precedents and prior statements that suggest that our action plan

28. How a Future Decision Could Be Announced

Case: Draft Iranian Statement on the Release
of American Hostages, 1980

During the past year, Iran has asked from the United States nothing more than that to which in our view Iran is entitled under international law, morality, custom, and the right of self-determination.

1. We wanted the world to be aware of the grievances which Iran suffered from more than 25 years under Mohammed Reza, who was actively supported by the United States Government;

2. We insisted that the Shah not be free to live abroad in luxury while the Iranian people suffered from the results of his reign;

3. We demanded that the United States Government fully accept the Iranian revolution;

4. We demanded a firm commitment from the United States Government never again to intervene in our internal affairs;

5. We demanded an end to economic warfare against the Iranian people;

6. We demanded assurance that no more punitive action would be taken against Iran by the United States;

7. We insisted that the United States cooperate in helping locate public funds wrongfully removed from Iran by the ex-Shah;

8. We demanded that the "nest-of-spies" — the U.S. Embassy compound from which the CIA aided the Shah — be closed and that future diplomatic facilities be established only by agreement with the Islamic Republic of Iran.

On all these points we have now succeeded. The ex-Shah has gone to face a judgment far more severe than any we could impose on him. The United States has now accepted all the above demands. The U.S. hostages no longer serve any useful purpose here, and they are accordingly being returned to their families.

As part of an effort to convince Iran and the United States that mediation might produce a successful conclusion to the protracted detention in Iran of U.S. diplomats, this draft statement and the one in Chart 29 were sent to both governments during the 1980 prenegotiations. Often one of the most persuasive documents we can prepare is a draft statement showing a decisionmaker how a proposed decision could be announced.

29. How a Future Decision Could Be Announced

Case: Draft United States Statement on the Release of American Hostages, 1980

I am pleased to announce that all American hostages held in Iran since last November have now left Iran on their way home to the United States.

The release of the hostages constitutes a great success for the principled steadfastness of the American people and of the hostages themselves. In connection with their release I would like to make three major points:

1. We paid no blackmail. The American people have shown that they will not be coerced. We refused to turn over the Shah; we refused to pay ransom of any kind. Iran is receiving no more than that to which they would have been entitled under our own interpretation of international law if they had never taken the hostages.

2. Iran has been punished. As the result of measures taken by the United States and other countries, Iran's economy is in a disastrous state. Its international prestige has never been lower. Domestically the government is beset by infighting and disarray. Thus, Iran has paid a high price for its outrageous action. In return, they have gotten nothing that they could not otherwise have obtained much sooner.

3. The stability of the region is more important than further punishment of Iran. Although Iran may deserve still more punishment, we must give higher priority to the United States' long-term security interests in that part of the world. Ending our dispute with Iran will strengthen the independence and security of all the peoples of the Gulf region and reduce the risk of Soviet intervention. While we must not forget the past — the courageous steadfastness of the hostages and the bravery of those who gave their lives trying to rescue them — we need now to look to the future.

Accordingly the Government of Iran has been informed that the official policy of the United States toward Iran shall be as follows, effective immediately:

Both this draft and the one in Chart 28 were written some six months before the hostages were freed. Their purpose was to help convince the two governments that despite their serious disagreements, there was a potential agreement that was in their mutual interest.

30. Political Constraints on Choice

Case: North American Free Trade Agreement, 1993

Decisionmaker: President Clinton

Substance of the decision: To support the North American Free Trade Agreement

The vulnerability of the proposed decision to political criticism:

Some potential critics:
Organized labor
Ross Perot
Environmental groups
Some congressional representatives

Attacks on the decision which they could possibly make:
"Americans will lose their jobs since American companies will relocate to Mexico."

"The agreement will not stop illegal immigration."

"American companies will face unfair competition."

"We will sink to their lower environmental standards."

"America will be at a disadvantage because Mexico won't enforce the labor provisions."

How he might present the decision most favorably:

Possible announcements:
"With the additional changes and side agreements, this agreement will help peoples in all countries."

"It will strengthen the Mexican economy and open its vast consumer market to U.S. producers."

"Increased trade means lower prices for American consumers."

Prior statements:
"Free trade with our neighbors will help the U.S. economy."

"The NAFTA agreement will make all parties better off in the long run."

Precedents:
The United States is a traditional supporter of free trade.

The United States is a member of GATT and has numerous bilateral free trade agreements around the world.

Principle:
Free trade is good for our economy.

As we formulate a yesable proposition, we will want to subject it to some political reality testing. A good way to appraise the political viability of a proposal is to write out who would criticize the decision, what they could be expected to say, how it might be announced, and some possible responses to the criticism.

is the right thing to do. It will also help to be able to articulate the principle which the proposed decision implements. This is basically what lobbyists do to convince representatives that voting for a specific proposal will sound good to their constituents.

As we formulate a yesable proposition and attempt to make it potentially acceptable to a decisionmaker on our side, the scope of the proposed decision often becomes smaller and smaller. We find ourselves wanting to propose a course of conduct involving many decisions over a period of time, yet coming to recognize that decisions are made one at a time. To some extent this concern can be met by pointing out that one advantage of making decision A is that it can be followed up with decisions B, C, and D. Another technique is to propose as the first decision a public speech (of which we could enclose a draft) that would include commitments to a course of action. An action plan doesn't result in action if it is never implemented. Our overall objective is to make ourselves more persuasive by presenting a way forward, not a problem.

6
Help Change the Game

Coping ad hoc with one conflict after another is an endless task — necessary, but endless. In order to move beyond a continuous search for one-shot solutions, we will want to improve the mechanisms for dealing with conflict. If we are tired of bailing water, maybe it is time to fix the pump. We will want to work on the international system in which individual conflicts are embedded. It is in our long-term interest both to play each hand well and also to improve the game.

If the techniques we have suggested are effective for influencing players in the game of nations, those same techniques should be effective for influencing those same players to create a new game. What is true for the post-Cold War international political system is true for domestic situations, whether we are concerned with governments, corporations, schools, or the family. The tools in our toolbox are equally applicable to the long-term task of improving the way the world routinely copes with its conflicting interests.

In order to think systematically about this task, we begin with the question: What, exactly, is wrong? Whether thinking of Bosnia, Kashmir, Somalia, Sudan, Nagorno-Karabakh, or any other violent dispute, the most prominent symptom we see is the failure of the mechanisms we have designed to manage international conflict. Institutions like the Organization of American States and their member governments tend simply to *react* to a violent situation, such as apparent Serbian aggression against Croatia or Bosnia, rather than to formulate a clear, future-oriented purpose which then guides their actions. In those cases where a purpose has been formulated, it is likely to be a one-shot "solution," which is rarely achievable. Rather than ask themselves how the system can best deal with ongoing conflicting interests, such as among ethnic groups, those in the international arena often look for a quick fix. Although drawing a new boundary among ethnic groups — groups that include many mixed marriages — will never be enough to put minority concerns to rest, that is the kind of "solution" that the international community is likely to pursue.

Instead of focusing their attention on the interests of those whose decisions they are trying to influence, governments, international organizations, nongovernmental organizations, and others are likely to start by asking themselves, "What shall *we* do?" They fail to focus on points of choice. Open letters on newspaper editorial pages or "working papers" from think tanks are often created without a particular decisionmaker in mind, and the net result can be the equivalent of shooting good ideas into space. If there is no decisionmaking entity to talk to, it is also unlikely that we can constitute one by decree. In Somalia, UNOSOM's attempts to set up "district councils" to implement development policy and build political institutions deemphasize the role of clan and subclan rivalries in that country — who will decide who serves on these councils? If decisionmaking units have been unable to transcend clan boundaries within districts before now, what has changed that would make these district councils different? It would seem more promising to persuade clan leaders to make better decisions before more ambitious administrative units can make sense, perhaps through promoting first-hand experiences of the advantages of interclan cooperation.

In voting for sanctions, proposing war crimes trials, or adopting resolutions condemning someone's behavior, members of an international organization rarely go through the exercise of asking how the message they are sending is likely to be heard by those to whom it is directed. This failure to understand the message as others will hear it can often be remedied by systematically considering their choice, by stepping into their shoes and considering how a proposal will likely sound to them. "Lay down your arms so we can try you for your atrocities against civilians" is unlikely to be a very compelling argument to a Serb partisan. If an international organization sees its purpose as expressing collective outrage, a public commitment to war crimes trials in advance of a ceasefire may fill the bill. If purposes are framed differently, however, more effective roles are available.

Through the behaviors just described, the international community time and again confronts those involved in a conflict with a further problem, rather than with a way out. They fail to propose a yesable proposition. The call for a Western military response to continuing war in Bosnia along the lines of the Gulf War's Operation Desert Storm does not address how massive air power can stop atrocities in mountainous regions where civilians and paramilitary soldiers mix freely, or answer the question who would define the objectives of such a mission and decide when they had been met. A yesable proposition demands a plan that is sufficient, realistic, and operational. Even two out of three is not good enough, as with the more limited military option for Bosnia of using NATO troops to take out the bridges there: While such a mission, if planned carefully, could be operational and realistic, it is surely not sufficient.

Running through the previous chapters of this book are many ideas that could explain why these kinds of failures are so widespread, and many suggestions for developing better strategies to avoid them. We want to look now at four diagnoses that seem particularly important:

(1) The poor design of third-party activities;
(2) Limited staff, limited skill;
(3) Constraints on officials; and
(4) The roles played by institutions.

How might these recurring problems be better managed?

The Design of Third Parties' Roles

Players who are not principals in a conflict can play a wide range of constructive roles. Third-party interventions can contribute to problem-solving by making sure that disputants attack the problem rather than each other, and by keeping the focus on interests rather than on positions. Some roles are purely administrative, such as the functions associated with hosting a Devising Session or a conference. Other roles engage the third party in the substance of the dispute.

In a world filled with ready-made dispute-resolution procedures, it is important to look beyond the labels of "alternative dispute resolution," "negotiation," "mediation," and "arbitration" when considering useful roles for third parties. Chart 31 illustrates a variety of roles that third parties can play, ranging from primarily process-oriented ones, such as hosting a diplomatic conference, to primarily substance-oriented ones, such as monitoring compliance after an agreement. In any action plan involv-

31. Some Third-Party Roles for Coping with a Conflict

Range of roles	Examples	Who might play them
Primarily process-oriented roles	Hosting a diplomatic conference	Another government
	Developing tools for the parties to use in diagnosing their conflict	Academic institutions
	Facilitating a brainstorming session	A trained facilitator
Mixed process and substantive roles	Holding a devising session to develop a range of options for the parties' consideration	A nonprofit foundation
	Facilitating a one-text procedure	A prominent international figure
	Providing peace-keeping forces to maintain a ceasefire while negotiations continue	The U.N. or a regional group such as the OAS
Primarily substance-oriented roles	Providing neutral evaluation of the merits of parties' claims	A professional association or specialized arbitration organization
	Providing a binding decision for outstanding issues in a dispute	The World Court

ing the participation of a third party, what is most important is to design a role for the third party that addresses the particular diagnosis of why a given conflict has not been settled. In September 1993 the PLO and Israel needed a symbolic occasion to cement their commitment to work with each other toward a comprehensive peace. Their leaders were also in need of something that would help explain to their respective constituents why each shook the other's hand. What was needed at that time is what President Clinton, as a third party, provided in an impressive ceremony on the lawn of the White House.

Making a Seven Elements analysis of a conflict can help a third party identify what most needs attention. If there is a shortage of creative options, the third party may want to host a brainstorming or Devising Session. If the parties have unrealistic assessments of their situation should the negotiation fail, a neutral evaluation of their walk-away alternatives — their BATNAs — may be indicated. If the parties cannot agree on relevant principles or criteria, a third party might recommend some, or it might work out an agreement to submit certain issues for adjudication.

One way in which third parties often try to assist the parties is in mediating between them. The mediation technique perhaps most commonly used by third parties — concession hunting — often fails because it does not address the underlying interests of the disputants that have impeded a settlement. Focusing on positions rather than interests, this strategy tries to persuade the parties to give up bits of their opposing positions piece by piece. The goal is to edge the parties' positions toward each other until they eventually converge. "Shuttle diplomacy" is an example of this concession-hunting approach. In the Sinai negotiations of 1973 to 1976, U.S. Secretary of State Henry Kissinger shuttled from capital to capital, asking first one party and then the other for a concession. Although his efforts did produce an agreed modus vivendi (at substantial cost to the United States), it failed to produce a peace agreement that met the underlying interests of either country.

Most players, in anticipation of this common strategy, adopt extreme positions from which they will later be able to make concessions without giving up anything important. Unfortunately, the "fat" that was originally included in order to pad a position is likely, through the process of public debate and commitment to one's constituents, to harden into "bone" that is now difficult to cut away.

The concession-hunting strategy directs attention to the comparative concessions made by each side and away from the best means of reconciling underlying interests. It suggests that interests are simply arguments used in support of positions, rather than the central concern that the parties must address. Concession-hunting also assumes that the optimal agreement is to be found at some hypothetical point perhaps midway between the opening positions of the two sides.

If we ask a decisionmaker for a concession, his currently perceived choice is likely to look something like that in Chart 32, and a rational answer to the mediator's request for a concession is likely to be "no" — or at least, "later." It is easy to see how this process encourages foot-dragging and haggling. This concession-hunting process tends to foreclose the possibility of generating creative options — the possibility that the pie can be enlarged through joint problem-solving.

A better process can change the choice. Rather than talking about two plans that reflect extreme partisan perceptions, it is usually better to talk about one plan that reflects some third party's judgment of what options might be acceptable to both sides. Consider how a lawyer might help two business professionals work out an agreement to become partners. One approach would be to ask each of them to draw up a separate plan, and then

32. Currently Perceived Choice

Created by a Concession-Hunting Mediator

"Shall I now make a concession from my stated position?"

Consequences if I say YES	Consequences if I say NO
− I have to decide what to give.	+ No problem deciding what to do.
− My hardliners will criticize me.	+ I maintain hardline support.
− I won't be able to take back what I have yielded.	+ By sticking to my position I support the reasonableness of my original demands.
− Whatever I give, this mediator will certainly ask for more.	+ I can wait to see what the other side does
− I start down a slippery slope.	+ The other side may make a concession.
− I have no idea where we will end up.	+ I can always give up something later.
BUT	**BUT**
+ I will not be blamed for a failure of the process.	− I may get blamed for the process not working.
+ There is a chance we might move toward agreement.	

to ask each for concessions until a common plan could be reached. A better way would be for the lawyer to listen to the two parties discuss their individual and joint interests, and then to produce a rough draft of points that might be included in a partnership agreement. This draft would not be "the lawyer's proposal" but rather an open draft for all to discuss. Each party would be asked for their criticisms of the draft, focusing on ways in which their interests might not be fully served. The lawyer would then prepare a revised and more detailed draft and again

33. Currently Perceived Choice

Created during the One-Text Process

"Shall I criticize this draft that the mediator has proffered?"

Consequences if I say YES	Consequences if I say NO
+ I lose nothing; I make no concession, no commitment	− I look uncooperative and antagonize the mediator.
+ Future drafts will better reflect my interests.	− I miss a chance to push this draft in a direction I would like.
+ I keep my options open.	− I am likely to face a worse draft tomorrow.
+ I can always say "no" later.	− I may be put under pressure to accept a later draft.

submit it for criticism. After a series of these successive drafts, the lawyer would finally say, "This is the best I can do," and ask for agreement.

Parties engaged in a conflict also need such a "business plan" of how they are going to deal with each other. Presenting disputants with a single draft that has been generated by the mediator and asking "What would be wrong with doing it this way?" is more likely to garner a constructive response than asking for a concession. It is typically difficult to give something away and to make commitments, especially when we are uncertain about what we will receive in return. It is always easy to criticize. The basic idea behind this One-Text Process is to design a new — and easier — series of choices for our decisionmaker. If a mediator asks for criticism of a new text, the choice faced by those on each side is now quite different and looks more like Chart 33. It presents a much easier decision to say yes to. Over the ensuing days and weeks, the mediator refines the draft by circulating among the parties, learning of concerns they may still have, and drafting new language designed to meet them as best he can. When the mediator feels that he cannot improve the draft any further — that it is fair, workable, and reconciles their conflicting interests as well as possible — he polishes the text and presents a final document to the parties for their approval. Each party's decisionmaker now faces a new choice which should look something like Chart 34.

The One-Text Process was used by President Carter and Secretary of State Cyrus Vance at the 1978 Camp David negotiations between President Anwar Sadat of Egypt and Prime Minister Menachem Begin of Israel. The U.S. negotiating team prepared some twenty-three consecutive drafts or redrafts of parts of a text over ten days, each responding to some point raised by a party. On the last day, President Carter decided that this was the best he could do and asked each party to agree. A few hours later, the Camp David Accords were signed.

Some differences between the widely used strategy of hunting for concessions and the One-Text procedure are summarized in Chart 35.

In some cases a mediator might want to employ a variation on the One-Text Process by producing two alternative drafts. These would not reflect partisan positions but, starting from different assumptions, would seek to meet as well as possible the interests of both parties. An architect, for example, might develop in parallel two alternative plans for his client, one a single-story house, the other a two-story house. Or a mediator working on a long-term settlement of the Palestinian-Israeli conflict might similarly develop in parallel drafts of two possible treaties. One would seek to meet Palestinian interests in acceptance, equality, self-government, and so forth without establishing a wholly independent sovereign Palestinian state. The other might start with such a state

34. Currently Perceived Choice

Faced at the End of the One-Text Process

"Shall I accept the mediator's final proposal?"

Consequences if I say YES

+ The commitment I am making is clear.

+ The document takes most of our interests into account.

+ It is a balanced, operational document carefully prepared by a competent neutral.

+ It is as good a proposal as we are likely to get.

+ Major issues in this dispute could be settled right now.

+ If the dispute does not end, the other side will be blamed.

BUT

− Some hardliners will criticize me.

− We do not get everything we want, and we forego the chance that we might possibly get something better.

Consequences if I say NO

− What happens next is unclear.

− The dispute with all its costs goes on.

− We will lose the efforts of this mediator; no other mediator is likely to volunteer.

− We are unlikely to get a better proposal.

− We will miss an opportunity that is unlikely to recur.

− We will be blamed for the mess.

BUT

+ I maintain hardliner support.

+ We keep open the unlikely possibility that we might later be offered something better.

and then consider how best to meet Israeli interests, particularly in security, through provisions about neutrality, mutual inspection, restrictions on weapons, and so on. If the parties became unable to choose between the two texts, they might go to the Security Council for its recommendation or decision.

The two-draft strategy is comparable to the "last best offers"

35. Two Ways of Generating a Draft Proposal

Concession-hunting	One-text
Ask the parties for their positions and proposals.	Ask the parties about their interests and concerns.
Focus discussion on each party's position.	Focus discussion on a single text aimed at reconciling conflicting interests and developing joint gains.
In turn, ask each party for a concession.	Ask each party to criticize the text wherever it fails to meet a legitimate interest.
Communicate the concessions obtained.	Prepare a revised single text in light of criticism and suggestions.
Repeat the process of pressing first one and then the other party for more concessions.	Repeat the process of revision until you have the best draft you can prepare.
Press one party or the other for a final concession to produce an agreement between the original positions of the parties.	Ask each party to accept the final draft if the other will. The final agreement may bear no relationship to the parties' original positions.

that are often advanced to settle the compensation disputes of professional baseball players. There, the player and the clubowner each submits a proposal to an arbitrator, who must select one or the other as being the fairer. Here, instead of staking out extreme positions, the disputants compete to make their preferred proposal the more reasonable. Parties sometimes find that once their interests have been met on all or virtually all other issues, an accommodation can be found on a previously irreconcilable difference.

A context where this process might be of use is in the ongoing struggle over the Canadian Constitution. A mediator might use this Two-Text Process to develop concurrently two possible agreements, one based on sovereign independence for Quebec and one on the assumption that Quebec would remain part of Canada. Each text would include details covering currency, trade, border control, immigration and movement, rights of English-speaking and French-speaking minorities in Quebec and elsewhere, the right to change citizenship, ownership of public buildings, financial aspects, transition arrangements, dispute-resolution clauses, military matters, police, and so forth.

One virtue of the Two-Text Process is that it directs the attention of the parties toward practical ways of handling practical questions — matters that are often obscured in debate over broad propositions like "independence." If the parties remain unable to choose between the two drafts, they might agree on a process for going forward, such as a referendum.

Skill of Staff

Although every international organization contains competent and dedicated people who work very hard, those offices that must deal with international conflicts tend to be underfunded, overloaded, and lacking in staff members who have been well-trained in the skills needed to cope effectively. And too often the governments, paramilitary groups, and guerrillas who are engaged in international violence similarly lack leaders and support staff who are skilled in the techniques of dealing peacefully with important differences.

Many of the people who play third-party roles in international conflicts are called upon not because of their conflict management skills but because of their political or international position. Sometimes there is a happy coincidence between the talents that enabled a mediator to acquire this international stature and the skills required to design and implement an effective process for conflict resolution. Sometimes not.

Being untrained, and feeling pressure to "get something done," mediators and negotiators tend to focus too soon on extracting some commitment from the parties, even if only an agreement in principle. Later efforts are then devoted to debating what was agreed upon rather than jointly exploring what ought to be agreed upon for the future.

Workshops can help. Training in negotiation and problem-solving gives potential mediators a low-risk environment in which to try out process techniques like the One-Text Process. Good training by itself does not "create" good mediators any more than good coaching, by itself, creates good athletes. But it can give talented people a systematic framework for analyzing things they are already doing that are working well, and for pinpointing areas of weakness. It also gives them an analytical framework to help them organize their own common sense and learn how to keep learning from experience.

Third parties in high-stakes, high-publicity roles will often be tempted to play to the grandstands. That is why it would be helpful if the constituencies in the grandstands were better informed about negotiation and skills for dealing well with conflict. The same workshops attended by lawyers and mediators can also benefit government officials, television news producers, and newspaper editors.

In addition to training current players and commentators on the international scene, we can turn our attention to potential players not yet in the picture — candidates for office, students in diplomatic academies and professional schools, or in colleges, high schools, and even primary schools. A sixth-grader wearing a "conflict resolver" T-shirt who has successfully mediated playground disputes is going to grow up with an empathic understanding of the challenges faced by the facilitator who intervenes in labor disputes or the diplomat who mediates international disputes. The sixth-grader may very well grow up to be one of those people.

Constraints on Third-Party Officials

Officials of governments and of organizations are necessarily restricted, both legally and politically, in what they can do. An international official is likely to consider that taking any initiative may be seen as an improper "intervention" in the internal affairs of some state. A government official is naturally reluctant to invite an international organization to become involved, for fear of what it may do. The result is often inaction at the very time that a third party might be most helpful.

Nonofficials are less constrained. Third parties can sometimes be more effective in resolving a conflict when they do not have a formally designated role. Sometimes behind-the-scenes counseling works best, where the third party is not "called in" by the disputants in a public and potentially embarrassing admission that assistance would be helpful.

At the Harvard Negotiation Project and the Conflict Management Group, our participation is sometimes solicited by just one faction of one side in a multiparty dispute — by a high-level official who took one of our courses, for example. At other times our participation is unsolicited; we occasionally approach a third party already involved in a particular international conflict and offer ideas or an informal workshop. In either scenario, we are negotiating our role as we go along. Disputants and third parties who have found our interventions to be of use often remark on the value of off-the-record analysis, brainstorming, and training. In many ways we cherish our role as international "meddlers" —

we believe that it enhances our effectiveness when it is clear that we are not beholden to one side or the other in a conflict.

The value of informal roles for third parties is perhaps best highlighted by what the *New York Times* has called the Oslo Connection in the Mideast Peace Pact signed in September 1993 by Yitzhak Rabin of Israel and Yasir Arafat, representing the Palestine Liberation Organization. At an otherwise uneventful academic conference in Tel Aviv in 1992, an opposition Labor member of the Israeli parliament became acquainted with the head of a Norwegian institute researching conditions in the Israeli-occupied territories (the West Bank, Gaza, and the Golan Heights). The two stayed in touch, and after the Labor party was voted into power, the M.P. became Israel's new Deputy Foreign Minister. The Norwegian academic renewed a standing offer to put his Israeli friend in touch with senior Palestinian officials. This offer led to Norway's becoming the back-channel passage for direct talks between the Israeli government and the PLO. As the *Times* described it: "In the months to follow, on elegant country estates and in ordinary hotel rooms, representatives of Israel and the PLO, enemies to the death for three decades, met secretly and stitched together a set of principles that is supposed to lead them out of their long struggle."

Participants in these behind-the-scenes negotiations emphasize that the informal atmosphere and the confidential nature of the discussions was a major factor in their success. Rather than high politics and formal diplomacy, "there was a more subtle combination of relaxed settings, home-cooked meals, mutual esteem, a knack for telling the right joke to ease a tense situation and, more important, an ability to keep secrets."*

It is also worth noting Norway's special role as third party.

---

*Clyde Haberman, "How the Oslo Connection Led to the Mideast Pact," *New York Times,* September 5, 1993.

"Norway could be a bridge between Israel and the PLO, not as a mediator but as an expediter, one graced with diplomatic sophistication, familiarity with the key figures and distance from the region and prying cameras."

Even without the platform of public office, academic appointment, or other institutional affiliation, each of us can often play an informal role as citizen diplomats. Just hosting a dinner for visitors from a nation with cool relations toward our own country can help break down partisan perceptions. Having hosted several such successful evenings, we could next consider inviting, say, an official from their Ministry of Culture to an informal get-together to which we would also have asked a steering committee member from our local symphony or repertory theater. Perhaps the foreign country in question has numerous cultural treasures and is interested in mounting a display of them that will tour various world capitals, attracting funding and generating publicity. We could put their relevant officials in touch with an official or curator from a third country, such as Egypt, that has already successfully executed such a tour.

Joining a local World Affairs Council can introduce us to visiting diplomats who are passing through our area for conferences and speaking engagements. Our focus need not be particularly political: As the example above suggests, we can concentrate on the international aspects of a cultural interest, such as music, theater, or cooking, just as easily as on a more overtly political concern such as children's rights, violence against women, or the transnational flow of technology. As an ordinary citizen, there is a great deal we can do, depending on whom we know or are willing to get to know, and how much energy we are willing to put into getting people together.

Finally, it is helpful to think about third-party roles separately from the intervention of a particular third party. Negotiating teams representing Japanese corporations regularly assign the role of observer to someone on their own team. This observer takes the role of the "fly on the wall," focusing not on the substance of the negotiations but rather on the process — on the way the negotiations are proceeding. Similarly, even when no third party is present, we can improve the quality of interactions between our side and other parties by specifically assigning functions that might be carried out by a third party to someone on our own side.

Roles of International Institutions

In this rapidly changing and increasingly interdependent world, many problems can be dealt with only by concerted action. No individual person or nation could ever handle global problems like hunger, drug trafficking, oil spills, ozone depletion, ethnic conflict, AIDS, or the transnational migration of populations. Such serious problems inevitably spawn some kind of international conference, usually with a permanent secretariat. A significant part of improving the substantive answers to continuing problems lies in improving the process through which international conferences, the United Nations General Assembly, and regional organizations cope with the problems before them. We can no longer afford to waste months on speeches and pious declarations of intent to be followed by years of haggling and concession-hunting.

The institutions for dealing with conflict are many: the United Nations, NATO, the Organization of American States, the Organization of African States, the Arab League, the Conference on Security and Cooperation in Europe, the European Community, the General Agreement on Trade and Tariffs, the specialized United Nations agencies, and some 160 or more ministries of foreign affairs. Most of these institutions seem to be caught up in the old game. Institutions tend to have roles that are sharply limited. Governments restrict the authority of international institutions, citing concerns about national sovereignty. Treaty-based institutions, such as the United Nations, the OAS, or the Council of Europe, are confined to roles agreed upon by treaty.

Barred from many useful activities, the role of an international institution in a conflict is likely to be formal and inflexible. With tightly constrained charters, institutions place significant emphasis on official votes, protocol, and authority. This practice is conducive to a search for options that are politically palatable, rather than effective. Debate over expanding the permanent membership of the U.N. Security Council is one example of this tendency. More attention is often paid to the effect on Germany and Japan of additional status than to the effect on other parties of Security Council resolutions.

Also, by their very nature, institutions sometimes escalate a problem simply by getting involved. For example, if the U.N. were to start talking with Hindu fundamentalists, Basque terrorists, or neo-Nazis in Germany or California, it might well encourage other splinter groups to become more violent in order to garner the same recognition. Given these constraints, it is not surprising that international institutions often fail to become involved until a conflict has grown too large to handle at low cost.

Some ways of making institutions more effective. It would be helpful to have some institutions that could get their hands on a problem at an early stage, follow a clear procedure, and confront the disputing parties with a yesable proposition. Ideally, we would like to set up standing committees or working groups within existing international institutions, groups that would be available to initiate off-the-record, unofficial dialogue. Violations or perceived violations of rules could be investigated and forward-looking remedial procedures be designed by ongoing working groups. Embryonic disputes might be easier to manage at an early stage before public positions are locked in and before the parties have escalated the conflict. Once a political or economic dispute is well under way, there are usually numerous obstacles to diplomats from the disputing countries sitting down together to exchange information, analyze the current situation, and brainstorm new approaches. When armed conflict is involved, obstacles to joint problem-solving are all but insurmountable. Nonpartisan analysts are rarely provided to conduct the kind of diagnostic and prescriptive processes suggested in this book, and the parties are rarely inclined to do so on their own. Disputants are seldom offered an opportunity to explore each other's interests or jointly to explore options. Small working groups within larger international institutions could change all that.

Humanitarian aid groups could also make a larger contribution to conflict resolution. They have traditionally considered conflict-prevention work "political," whereas providing food and medicine in conflicts around the world has been accepted as nonpolitical. There are many circumstances where these organizations, equipped with clear guidelines and well-trained personnel, could use their presence and involvement to help manage disputes more effectively. Facilitating talks, hosting a working meeting, or developing tools for the parties to use in diagnosing their conflict can be as neutral — and as helpful — as providing food and medicine.

We might also consider entirely new mechanisms for third-party involvement. For example, an international roster of nongovernmental Dispute Resolution Counselors might be set up to give third parties some legitimacy in the eyes of disputants and modest funding to target incipient problems on their own initiative. Each counselor might be able to undertake constructive dialogue with the disputing parties and get some kind of third-party process under way. Such a roster could include former diplomats and government leaders, judges, and academics. The roster could be extensive and varied. A small central staff of analysts and investigators might be available to prepare confidential background reports for the members of the roster. A staff might also be set up to offer training in problem-solving and conflict management for diplomats and government officials.

Is This a Yesable Proposition?

This chapter analyzes some existing mechanisms for coping with conflicts. In terms of our Four-Quadrant Analysis, we have covered Quadrant II — diagnosing what may be causing difficulties — and Quadrant III — advancing some general proposals. But if the ideas in this book are sound, we hope we have shown that this is not enough.

For us to be able to improve the way the system works, we will need to follow our own advice much further. We need to understand why a decisionmaker is not already acting as we would like. We will want to step into the shoes of a decisionmaker and consider how the ideas in this chapter might look, for example, to a hardworking U.N. or government official whose phone is ringing off the hook day after day. The currently perceived choice of such a person might well look like that suggested in Chart 36. If so, it should be no surprise that he or she is not actively changing the system.

This is where you come in. Having formulated the purpose of improving the system, and now understanding perhaps more clearly why the system, with all its drawbacks and limitations, continues as it does, we all have a basis for further work. We will, for example, want to focus on a point of choice, generate fresh ideas, formulate advice, and present someone with a yesable

36. Currently Perceived Choice

Case: Official Faced with a Suggestion to Change His or Her Approach to Coping with Conflict

"Shall I now decide to do things differently, as suggested in *Beyond Machiavelli?*"

Consequences if I say YES	Consequences if I say NO
− I will have no peer support.	+ All my colleagues will support me.
− They may laugh at my jargon about BATNAs and Yesable propositions.	+ I know the language.
− I really don't know just how to do it; I would not know how to start.	+ I know well what I'm doing.
− I take on even more work on top of my existing overload.	+ I can easily explain why we do things the way we do.
− It would be quite risky to try out some of these ideas.	+ Doing what I do is hard work but low risk.

proposition that meets their interests as well as our own. Although we describe ways of using all these ideas, nowhere do we suggest that writing a book — or reading one — is enough. While having on hand a systematic approach to influencing others should help, there is a lot left to be done.

Conclusion: Ask a Different Question

Conflict is inevitable. It will not disappear, nor can it be ignored. For better or for worse, we will have to cope with conflicting interests as long as we live. Before one dispute or crisis is apparently put to rest, another appears. Short-term food aid to Ethiopia is followed by a crisis in nearby Somalia. And ignoring desperate situations elsewhere in the world in the hope that they will not affect us is becoming less and less tenable. An epidemic, a dockstrike, an oil spill, or anarchy in one country quickly affects those in others. Today, a citizen in the developed world can no more ignore the problems of poorer nations than could a first-class passenger on an oceanliner say, "Don't worry; the leak is down in Third Class."

As children we are often taught not to argue, that it is wrong to quarrel, even that it is wrong to disagree. As adults, this often translates into behavior that seeks to avoid conflict, that tries to smooth over differences or sweep them under the rug. Neither response is an effective way of dealing with interests that genuinely conflict. Becoming a "conflict avoider" will often cause our interests to suffer. A hurried resolution is also unlikely to meet interests as well as some more carefully considered course of conduct.

Fortunately, conflict is not all bad. Differences can be a source of value. The fact that we have different priorities may mean that each of us can attain something important to us without injury to anything important to someone else. And in dealing with conflict, people are likely to be highly motivated, innovative, and energetic. If it is "the squeaky wheel that gets the grease," it may be wise to squeak. Because of the conflict over the North American Free Trade Agreement with Mexico, environmental standards in both Mexico and the United States will get more attention. This may well lead to a better long-term process for dealing with environmental issues than would have been the case if the trade agreement had been ratified without dissent. Increased attention can lead to greater creativity and toward something closer to an optimal agreement. If Pakistan and India had not had a dispute over their rights to the waters of the Indus River, the opportunity for joint development with the help of the World Bank might not have arisen.

Coping well with conflict also tends to strengthen a working relationship and to improve the ability of parties to deal with future differences. Working well together can turn adversaries into partners. Such changes have been common in the history of U.S. foreign relations. With each of several former enemies — Great Britain, Canada, Mexico, Spain, Germany, and Japan — the United States has now developed a constructive working relationship. While an immediate goal may be to improve the way our side deals with their side, a focus on process tends to leave us both on the same side.

To bring about such change, we have to be open — not simply open to new answers, but open to asking different questions.

Doing better is not a matter of producing good answers out of thin air, but a matter of asking a series of questions which are likely to result in coping more skillfully with an endless flow of conflicting interests. This book is not a book of answers and solutions. Every tool is intended to ask questions or to stimulate better questions.

Better questions are not about who is right and who is wrong, or about one-shot solutions, but about the process for dealing with conflicting views about right and wrong, and for dealing with the inevitable changes that lie ahead. If you are coping with a conflict, you might find it a useful exercise to go through the book writing down on the left-hand side of a page some questions that you have typically asked yourself in the past, and on the right-hand side some different questions that you might want to ask yourself in the future. For example, instead of starting with the question, "What shall I do?" you might want to start with such questions as "What would I like someone else to do?" "Why haven't they done it already?" And "What could I do that would make it easier for them to do it?"

It is not enough, however, simply to ask ourselves different questions. It is others whom we would like to influence, and we are undoubtedly going to want to change the questions that we have been asking of them.

As you know by now, we think process is important — the process for dealing with conflict, and particularly the process for producing good questions about how to deal with conflict. If we are right, the quest for better and better questions is going to be endless.

Although years in gestation, the tools in this book and the questions they ask are really just a start. If at any time a question posed seems misguided or unhelpful, ask a different question. We are sure there are many better questions out there just waiting to be asked.

Acknowledgments

Producing this book has been a team effort. The ideas and tools we offer have been developed and refined through years of teaching and advising. We have benefited from brainstorming sessions, early drafts of course materials, thoughtful criticism, and administrative and clerical assistance contributed by a great many people. We found that in writing the book we were constantly testing our own process—and the usefulness of the advice we offer—by applying it to ourselves.

Bruce Patton wrote many of the course materials on which early drafts of this book were based. Several of the charts and tools he designed with Roger also benefited from William Ury's good ideas. Wayne Davis, then an Associate Director of the Harvard Negotiation Project, got Liz involved in turning this "tool box" into a book. The dozens of teaching fellows who helped present these ideas to hundreds of Harvard undergraduates in the course Coping with International Conflict have been especially helpful. We particularly wish to thank those teaching fellows who took time to edit, review, and criticize chapters in addition to their classroom responsibilities. Diana Chigas, Andrew Clarkson, Wayne Davis, Peter Engel, Brian Ganson, Paul Mayer, and Robert Ricigliano made this a much better book by distilling their teaching experience for us. We offer a special thank-you to Paul Mayer, now in the Foreign Service, who took the course as an undergraduate and then went on to teach it as an associate at the Negotiation Project, eventually serving as Head Teaching Fellow. His hundreds of hours of work both improved the book and helped the authors to direct their energies effectively.

Michael Moffitt's careful research has saved us from several factual errors; Steven Isko and Lee Levison have been generous with their time and editorial suggestions. We are grateful to Lori Britton and Sheila Blake for providing faultless administrative assistance in addition to their many other responsibilities.

Our students first led us to make this a general-interest book by requesting copies of our working drafts for their parents and friends. Katherine Felsen, Elissa Gootman, William Jackson, Debbie Katzenellenbogen, Kathaleen Kelly, Mira Kothari, Matthew Lane, Gail Lebow, and Peter Schlactus—all former CWIC students—helped with research and made useful comments. We continue to be inspired by the examples of 18- and 19-year-olds who have received invitations and job offers from officials to whom they had written as part of the CWIC course.

Our editor at Harvard University Press, Susan Wallace Boehmer, offered invaluable insights into how these ideas might be communicated more clearly and was gracious about working within tight time constraints. Thanks also to Dr. Aida Donald, Editor-in-Chief and Assistant Director of the Press, whose enthusiasm for the project brought the book, and us, home to Harvard.

Jeffrey Wing and Alan Price of Conflict Management, Inc.,

helped us design our collaboration and select the publisher by facilitating a "One-Text" Process among the authors. This tool—described in Chapter 6—helped synthesize interests and clarify trade-offs in a constructive way; we can now vouch for its effectiveness as consumers as well as producers. Jeff and Alan's skill, patience, and good humor were much appreciated, and made a good process better. Many other people at CMI helped develop the ideas in this book over several years.

Brian Ganson and William Jackson, mentioned briefly above, have made such substantial contributions to the text in its final stages that they could accurately be termed coauthors. Brian, our editor at the Negotiation Project, was lured to this task with the representation that the book just needed a "final reader" to tighten the prose. He reconceptualized the core of the book, cut the length in half, and completely reorganized the text. As he noted, we needed to separate the "truly essential from the merely interesting." It is our readers who owe the most to Brian. If this is a short book with clear ideas, that is in large part because of his efforts.

William Jackson is in a class by himself. A CWIC alumnus, he came to the Negotiation Project as Roger's assistant and has worn every hat and played every role it is possible to play in the production of a manuscript. He has collaborated on the creation of new material, especially the charts; he has helped polish the text while acting as liaison with Harvard Press; he has proposed agendas, acted as a soundingboard, arranged conference calls among the authors, and kept the three of us focused, without ever once being daunted by the burdensome administrative work necessary to a project of this scope. This book would be in a file drawer today were it not for William's efforts.

Finally, we wish to thank our spouses, Caroline Fisher, Kurt

Borgwardt, and Rodd Schneider. Carrie put up with Roger's working during vacations; Kurt and Rodd (barely) tolerated Liz and Andrea's working during their respective honeymoons. We are grateful for their forbearance—they have taught us a great deal about the value of coping well with conflict.

— R.F., E.K., A.K.S.

List of Charts